The Career Professional's Guide to Research

How to Plan and Deliver Excellence in Research

Emma Bolger

The Career Professional's Guide to Research

This first edition published in 2025 by Trotman, an imprint of Trotman Indigo Publishing Ltd, 18e Charles Street, Bath BA1 1HX

© Trotman Indigo Publishing Ltd 2025

Author: Dr Emma Bolger

British Library Cataloguing in Publication Data
A catalogue record for this book is available from the British Library.

Paperback ISBN 978-1-911724-59-9
eISBN 978-1-911724-60-5

All rights reserved. This book is sold subject to the condition that it shall not, by way of trade or otherwise, be lent, resold, hired out or otherwise circulated without the publisher's prior written consent in any form of binding or cover other than that in which it is published and without a similar condition including this condition being imposed on the subsequent purchaser. No part of this publication may be reproduced, stored in a retrieval system or transmitted in any form or by any means, electronic and mechanical, photocopying, recording or otherwise without prior permission of Trotman Indigo Publishing.

Every effort has been made to trace copyright holders and to obtain their permission for the use of copyright material. The publisher apologises for any errors or omissions, and would be grateful to be notified of any corrections that should be incorporated in future editions of this book.

The authorised representative in the EEA is Easy Access System Europe Oü (EAS), Mustamäe tee 50, 10621 Tallinn, Estonia.

Printed and bound in the UK by Ashford Colour Ltd.

 All details in this book were correct at the time of going to press. To keep up to date with all the latest news and updates and to access the online resources that accompany this book, use this QR code or visit www.trotman.co.uk/pages/the-career-professionals-guide-to-research-resources

Contents

About the author	vii
Acknowledgements	ix
Foreword	xi

Chapter 1 The importance of career practitioner-led research — 1
- Why *your* research matters — 1
- Who is this book for? — 2
- A note about terms — 2
- About this book/how to use this book — 3

Chapter 2 What makes a good researcher? — 5
- The core professional values we expect from career development professionals, and how these translate into research — 5
- The identity of a career practitioner-researcher — 8
- Research as a National Occupational Standard — 9

Chapter 3 What makes a good research topic? — 15
- Defining career practitioner-led research — 15
- Defining a career research project — 16
- Starting small and close to home — 16
- Locating your research project — 17
- Quality assurance in career guidance — 19
- The bigger picture — 21
- Checklist: Your early project plan — 23

Chapter 4 Ethics — 25
- What is 'ethical research'? — 25
- Beyond compliance — 25
- Evidencing ethical standards — 26
- Ethics training — 27
- Formal (and informal) ethical review — 27
- Key ethical principles — 28
- Codes of practice — 30
- The UK Career Development Institute Code of Ethics — 31
- AGCAS: A code of ethics for higher education career professionals — 36
- Key principles — 36
- Mitigating and responding to challenges of impartiality — 39
- Responding to an ethical challenge — 40

Chapter 5 Obtaining information and using valid data   43
Using sources of information to justify your project   43
A literature-first approach   44
Exploring sources   46

Chapter 6 Research methods: Quantitative and qualitative data collection tools   49
Becoming more research-engaged   49
Secondary data research   49
Primary data collection   51
Data types   51
Sample size, targets and response rates   52
Data collection: Popular methods   54
Interviews   54
Focus groups   55
Online data collection: Surveys   57
Surveys: Key points to remember   57
Survey design   58
Pilot surveys   59
Planning for inclusive data collection   60
Participant information and informed consent   62

Chapter 7 Writing a research proposal/plan   63
Plans and proposals   63
Aims, objectives and research questions   63
Methodology   65
Indicative timeline   66
Preventing a crisis/needs analysis   66
Output   66
Checklist   67
Writing your proposal   68

Chapter 8 Conducting and troubleshooting your project   71
Consider a research project journal   71
When your research meanders (and why that is not a problem!)   72
Troubleshooting   72
Keeping to (borrowed) time   72
Support if you are disabled, have a learning difficulty or are neurodivergent   73
Losing confidence   73
Support networks: Communities of practice   74

Chapter 9 Bringing it together: Findings and data analysis — 77
- Presenting your story — 77
- Data analysis — 77
- Qualitative analysis — 78
- Quantitative analysis — 79
- Data visualisation — 81
- Hypothesis testing — 82
- Assumptions — 82
- Software — 82
- Discussing your findings — 84

Chapter 10 Dissemination (sharing and promoting your research) — 89
- Who is your audience? — 89
- Moving away from the idea of a hierarchy — 90
- Where do we see career research? — 91
- You have done all this research, and now they want to charge you for it? — 92
- Presentations: Conferences and symposia — 92
- Pitching your idea — 93
- Seeking publication — 95
- Writing to a set brief — 96
- Self-publishing: Blogs and writing for LinkedIn — 99
- Running an online session — 100
- Promotion in an online world — 101
- Where and how do you want to share your work? — 102
- Formal and informal presentations — 102
- Professional articles, reports and websites — 103
- Self-publishing — 103
- Academic journals — 103
- Formal and informal presentations — 104
- Professional articles, reports and websites — 105
- Academic journals — 105

Chapter 11 Where next? Developing your role as a researcher — 107
- Continuous professional development: Formal study in research methods — 107
- Master's level study — 108
- Academic roles — 109
- Doctoral research — 111

  Related roles in research organisations   114
  Working in collaboration   114

General resources   117
Project templates   125

About the author

Dr Emma Bolger has over 20 years' experience working in the career sector as a practitioner and lecturer, most recently as the Programme Leader of the MSc Career Guidance and Development at the University of the West of Scotland. Emma's work and research focuses on equality and inclusion, diversity and accessibility. She completed her PhD in 2021 on the topic of Gender and Career Decision Making.

Emma lives in Scotland with her husband and three children. When she isn't working you can find her in the gym, exploring the wonderful Scottish outdoors or at home playing board games. Emma is an active volunteer in the area of parental involvement in education, with a particular focus on additional support needs.

If you would like to find out more about Emma's work, you can visit her website at www.emmabolger.co.uk

Acknowledgements

Firstly, thank you to Claire Johnson and Siobhan Neary for the video call during which we discussed the need for a book on practitioner-led research for career professionals. It has been a joy to work with the team at Trotman to bring that idea to fruition, with the support of my brilliant editor Alexandra Price.

To the many career professionals who showed their support and shared their insights and experiences on research: thank you; this book would not be what it is without your input.

This book is dedicated to my family: my husband Eamonn, son Fiachra and daughters Rona (AKA, the original 'careers baby' who ran the conference circuit with me in 2019) and Una.

Foreword

The centrality of research to the career development profession has been growing in recognition in recent years, not just within the confines of academia but also at the 'coal face' of day-to-day career development practice. The book you are holding, authored by one of the profession's leading researchers, Emma Bolger, represents an indispensable guide to research for those in any field of career development practice who are considering embarking on this burgeoning field.

Recognising that many careers professionals will approach research for the first time with trepidation – perhaps assuming that they need a PhD and an academic job in order to even consider research – Bolger starts this book by emphasising how well placed such professionals are to be able to produce high-quality research. Assuming no special knowledge on the part of the reader, Bolger goes on to outline the qualities of a good researcher, what characterises a good research topic, and how to conduct research ethically, amongst other, equally vital topics.

Jargon-free, readers will find this book accessible and practical in equal measure. Bolger helpfully provides practical activities to reinforce learning on the various topics covered, and clearly relates chapter content to the variety of ethical frameworks, benchmarks and competencies that guide their everyday practice. As such, this book does an admirable job of situating research as a core activity of career development practice, rather than something peripheral to the 'core business' of careers work.

Having thoroughly covered the basics of careers research for those unfamiliar with the activity, Bolger does not stop there. The latter stages of the book help the reader look ahead to how they may wish to develop and disseminate their research, offering a comprehensive overview of the range of platforms on which readers can publish their research, as well as ways in which readers can enhance their skills through CPD or even postgraduate study.

This book fills a vital gap in the career development literature, not only offering a truly accessible and comprehensive manual for beginning researchers but also a very helpful resource for experienced researchers. A foundational work in its topic, it should be essential reading for careers professionals working in every part of our sector.

Dr Oliver Jenkin PGCE RCDP, NICEC Fellow
Senior Professional Development and Standards Manager at the CDI
and Editor of the CDI's magazine, Career Matters
May 2025

Chapter 1
The importance of career practitioner-led research

Many practitioners want to use their workplace as the basis for research in the career development sector but are unsure of where to start. You might have a specific client group whose needs you would like to better understand, or a project to evaluate. You might want to unpick some fundamentals of practice or propose a new way of working, but you feel under-confident and do not know where to begin.

This book will explain why it matters that you conduct research, and guide you through how to plan, deliver and share your robust, ethically sound research with the right audience. Throughout, there will be helpful tips from fellow practitioners and stakeholders, and easy-to-work-on tasks to help you progress through your practitioner-researcher journey.

Why *your* research matters

You probably have some idea already of why there is a need for frontline practitioner-led research. You have picked up this book because you want to develop the skills to do your research well and share your findings with the right audiences. Stage by stage, I will guide you through that process.

The start of a research project inevitably involves many questions: What data will be analysed? Who will be involved? How long will it take? Before reaching this practical stage, let us first take a moment to understand and justify why, as career advisers, career consultants, human resource specialists, employability advisers and all other related career-work practitioners, we not only have the urge to undertake new research but are best positioned to do so.

Consider these big questions:

- Why, as a career specialist, do you want to conduct research?
- Why are you the right person to explore the issues you see in career work?

You should trust your instincts here. The answer to both questions is that career professionals are in a unique position to conduct research, and their perspective, developed from working in frontline practice, adds value.

You may feel daunted about starting out and evidencing your credibility as a researcher. Research must demonstrate purpose and relevance, stand up to scrutiny, be truthful and ethically compliant. The journey to achieving this might seem intimidating at first, but you are well placed to conduct research, and your perspective is highly beneficial to a wide range of stakeholders.

Practitioner-led research is an important, indeed vital, part of the research landscape. I hope that through reading and engaging with the topics covered in this book, you will learn new skills and go on to produce research that makes a difference to everyday practice within our sector and to the lives of the individuals we work with.

Who is this book for?

Anyone involved in career work, in its broad forms:

- School career adviser.
- Private career practitioner.
- Career consultant in higher or further education.
- Career leader.
- Employability adviser.
- Career teacher.
- Tutor/Lecturer.
- Career guidance student.
- Vocational coach.
- Training provider.
- Human resources adviser.
- Learning and development adviser.
- Doctoral researcher.

A note about terms

Throughout the book, I will refer to career practitioner-led research. This is an all-encompassing and flexible term to describe any form of research that is undertaken by professionals engaged in career work. Similar terms include practitioner-engaged research, practitioner enquiry, practice-based research, applied research, practitioner driven research. These are definitions that are used across professions where it is common to see research that is inspired, led and/or conducted by frontline staff.

When I talk about research by practitioners, I do not refer only to research on or about practice; your topics can and should encompass more than what happens in individual or group career practice (although focusing directly on the tools, techniques and methods of career information advice and guidance are indeed valid and interesting research projects).

About this book/how to use this book

This book offers a framework to help you plan and conduct your research and then promote your research and further your skills. The book is written so that you can read it cover to cover and come back later to dip in and out of the sections you need to support your research.

In each chapter, you will find practical activities to enable you to work on your own research project and insights from fellow practitioner-researchers.

At the end, you will find a **General resources** section containing details of a range of resources that will be useful to a practitioner-researchers like yourself. There is also a **Project templates** section offering helpful guidance on how to structure and word key documents, such as your research project proposal and participant information document.

I have one practitioner quote that I want to start with, as it covers everything that I hope this book brings to you as a new researcher:

'Doing a research project is something I would love to do but imposter syndrome definitely kicks in. How would I be taken seriously and how to get an idea to become a research project – I don't know where to start!'
Caroline Graham, Schools-based Career Adviser & HE coordinator

Let's get started together now! I hope you enjoy the book.

Chapter 2
What makes a good researcher?

Reflecting on our professional values is a great route to understanding why we want to engage with research. Professional behaviours, often supported by our professional memberships and affiliations, underpin the work that we conduct in the career sector, and this must extend to any research that we undertake.

I will talk in detail about codes of practice, ethics and research in Chapter 4, but for now, let's look at the wider professional values that we are expected to uphold as practitioners, and, in turn, as practitioner-researchers.

The core professional values we expect from career development professionals, and how these translate into research

It is in our core professional values that I believe we demonstrate why practitioners can be intuitively good researchers. Our professional standards underpin not only our practice but any research we undertake, in conjunction with the development of practical research skills.

Although not all career researchers will be members of a relevant professional body, it is important to be mindful of the expectations of the sector. This is especially important if you will be looking to professional bodies to support and share your research upon completion.

The research competence of a career development professional has a bearing on the reputation of the career development sector. While lax values in a researcher risk bringing the sector into ill repute, the converse, a rigorous dedication to robust and ethical practice, can promote the sector, highlighting how the career development researcher-practitioner has unique strengths which can be harnessed for wider benefit. The abilities of the career development practitioner can also be well-utilised in the methods of the research (see Chapter 5).

Independent thinking

As a researcher, it is likely you will be working independently on a self-directed project. Unless your research is supported and directed by your employer, you may feel like you are taking a step into the unknown and doing so alone. As an independent researcher, you may benefit from thinking about some of the principles that underpin self-employment to guide you. I will cover all of these points in later chapters.

Thinking like a freelancer:

- Self-directing your research: getting stuck in and doing it yourself;
- Committing your time and energy (monetary commitment may be minimal, but there are capital resources required);
- New learning;
- Following rules and regulations, particularly around the ethical protocols of research;
- Carving out a niche for yourself or creating a profile/identity as a researcher;
- Making connections and networking with fellow researchers;
- **Remembering never to undersell what you are capable of!**

 PRACTITIONER QUOTES

I asked people working in the career sector 'What makes a good researcher?' and here are some of their replies:

'A great careers researcher takes something they are curious about and builds on this curiosity in a structured way. They gather evidence and insights to explore their topic, analyse and reflect on the evidence they gather, and are open and willing to challenge themselves and their assumptions in the conclusions they come to.'

Dr Rosie Alexander, Researcher

'I appreciate researchers who are working in the field, and are applying their research into practice, to see what genuinely works, and in what circumstances.'

Kath Dunn, Career Consultant

'Someone who is knowledgeable and explores all perspectives.'

Anonymous

'Awareness of the impact of research on career guidance and policy and also real world awareness – academic theory is important, but the application of theory/research in day to day work/sector is equally important.'

HE Career Practitioner

'I think a good careers researcher has the balance of topic related skills and an analytical/enquiring mindset. Good careers research can come from many careers related professional areas such as those focused on employability skills development, career choice theory, employer recruitment methods, information provision or labour market trends but all have to be passionate about the subject and knowledgeable.'

HE Career Practitioner

'A passion for enhancing career practice and focus on key stakeholders, especially the client.'

Dr Tania Lyden, Assistant Professor (Higher Education Lecturer)

'Be ready to listen to alternative points of view – everyone's opinion is valuable, if only to consolidate your own thinking.'

Jillian Millar, Career Guidance Practitioner

'(An) open mind, active listening, willingness to co-create research not pushing a certain agenda from the start and wanting research to be useful for practice.'

Helena Landstedt Wennberg, Career Guidance Professional

'I think that there are different qualities that are desirable for different types of research, ranging from experience on the front line of the sector to academic discipline. What I think makes a researcher in our sector stand out is when they are able to combine both of these, so making their research accessible to everyone from those with no prior knowledge to experts. I also think that the best research comes from those who are genuinely passionate about the topic they are researching and want to make a positive impact for those who perhaps have been underrepresented or not heard in the past.'

Natalie Freeman, Employability Skills Award Manager

'Patience, focus, a strong interest in what is being researched, integrity, critical thinking, curiosity, resilience and the ability to take feedback on board.'

Emma Hill, Career Development Consultant

The identity of a career practitioner-researcher

What does a practitioner-researcher look like? Someone who is curious, keen to learn, keen to contribute, keen to make a difference. They are someone we can trust and have faith in.

A career practitioner-researcher is someone who:

Is keen to learn
Learning how to conduct research is a great form of continuous professional development (CPD) and can form part of a continuous cycle of learning. Learning how to do research can give you the opportunity to engage in structured CPD, and research training can enable you to re-engage with formal, academic learning.

Is research-engaged
A key part of our professionalism is an ongoing engagement with research, to maintain knowledge, be informed on contemporary issues and learn about best practices. Before you start working on your own projects, you should spend time looking at research produced by your fellow practitioner-researchers from a researcher's perspective: What methods did they use to conduct their research? How might your ideas build on previous research? What theories are being used to direct research? What are the main debates that are taking place?

Is competent
This may seem a simplistic summary, but this is the basic starting point; capability and expertise must be evident. Even if you do not go on to conduct research yourself, it is very much worth understanding what good research looks like so you can scrutinise the work of others and commission the right people to produce research for you.

Advocates for our profession
Research enables us to promote and validate the work that we do every day.

Is astute and critical
You have reviewed the research and spotted a gap, or perhaps you have reviewed existing research and found it to be biased, limited or without application to your specific context . . . and just like that, you have a research project waiting to emerge.

Wants to make a contribution
Research enables us to make a broader contribution to the career guidance and development sector. Career work is rooted in facts and reliable evidence about career opportunities, labour market contexts, decisions, support and the way we conduct our practice. It is natural to want to contribute to the body of evidence that we consult every day in our work.

Expects the unexpected
No two days are the same when it comes to working with career clients, and the research journey will have as many twists and turns as any individual's life. You might have a hunch about where your research journey might take you, but you should expect to have every expectation upended and learn more about your topic as you go along. Be open-minded and impartial as you embark on your research journey!

Advocate! Are you a service manager who is commissioning research?

Are you contracting individuals or organisations to conduct career research? Consider involving practitioners, as well as policy bodies, think tanks and academics from the get-go – not only as participants or to help test/trial new ideas as part of your project. If research is to be practice-focused, you need practitioners involved from the start.

Build! Establish a research culture in your organisation

How can your organisation demonstrate that you value practitioner-led research? To enable practitioner-researchers to emerge, there are some easy steps you might take to build confidence. Could you . . .

- organise a regular research-discussion forum?
- fund staff to attend research events and conferences?
- offer funding to staff to engage in research training?
- support small-stage practitioner-led research in your organisation?
- invite practitioner-researchers to discuss their research?
- partner with any academic researchers to mentor staff?
- partner with any other organisations to form a community of practice for research or research network?

Research as a National Occupational Standard

In the UK, National Occupational Standards (NOS) exist for career development work. (While we are here, I will highlight that the NOS not only indicate the expectations of professionals in the sector but are a great resource for helping you to identify your own CPD needs overall.)

One of the **NOS, CLDCD17: Plan and undertake research**, relates specifically to the expectations we have of practitioner-researchers in relation to career research. The NOS cover Performance Criteria (what you must be able to do to conduct career research) and Knowledge and Understanding (the skills of conducting research).

The current **NOS CLDCD17: Plan and undertake research** is described as follows:

'This standard is about planning and undertaking research on local, national or international career development information and practice to improve the information and resources available to individuals and practitioners. Research could be about theory and practice in career development or the learning and labour market.'[1]

NOS CLDCD17 is reproduced in full as part of the following activity with kind permission of Skills Development Scotland. NOS CLDCD17 can be found on the NOS database www.ukstandards.org.uk/en/nos-finder.

Activity

To help you to reflect on how your existing knowledge, skills and experience put you in a strong position to embark on research, here is a reflective checklist for you to consider the extent to which your existing skills and abilities as a budding researcher map onto the NOS. You can find an example completed by a career practitioner-researcher and a blank version of the checklist to fill in with your own answers in the **online resources** that accompany this book. To access, use the QR code or visit the web address at the start of this book.

---

1 Source: https://cldstandardscouncil.org.uk/wp-content/uploads/CareerDevelopment NOS2021.pdf

NOS CLDCD17: Plan and undertake research

Complete this table to consider how your existing skills in your practice map easily onto the expectations of a researcher. The first row has been filled out by a career practitioner-researcher as an example.

	Performance criteria	Do I do this in my work already? How?
1.	Explain the research brief, the information required, how it will be used and how it needs to be presented when planning research.	*This feels similar to initiating a new piece of work (e.g. a service development, piece of learning etc) and completing the initial 'project initiation document' to set out the scope/parameters.* *I regularly scope research or consultancy projects by clarifying aims, audiences and preferred formats. I've been asked to include international and academic perspectives in guidance documents, and to summarise findings for audiences such as policy teams or senior leaders.*
2.	Identify, and secure access to, resources that enable accurate analysis of information collected.	
3.	Apply appropriate and ethical research methods and strategies to obtain information when undertaking research.	
4.	Collect data relevant to the aims of the research plan.	
5.	Collate, analyse and present information to meet the research brief.	
6.	Maintain records of sources, search techniques and strategies together with the results of your research that comply with relevant legislation and organisational procedures.	
7.	Analyse and disseminate outcomes.	
8.	Identify possible further sources of information and evaluate for relevance and appropriateness.	

(Continued)

NOS CLDCD17: Plan and undertake research (Continued)

	Performance criteria	Do I do this in my work already? How?
9.	Evaluate research activity and plan improvements for future research as required.	
10.	Act in ways that adhere to the ethical practice required within your organisation or profession.	
11.	Challenge any prejudice, use of stereotypes, discrimination and unethical or oppressive behaviour.	
12.	Promote inclusivity, diversity and equality of opportunity.	
13.	Maintain confidentiality and security of individual information that meets relevant legal requirements and organisational policies.	

	Knowledge and understanding	Do I have this skill? How do I use it?	What do I still need to learn?
1.	Legal, organisational and policy requirements relevant to your role and the activities being carried out.	*I'd say I used to have a better grip on this when I was very experienced in previous roles but less so perhaps in my current roles.* *I interpret legislation and policy when reviewing or advising on practice.*	*Stay current with changes to data protection and equality law.*
2.	Relevant ethical principles and codes of professional ethical practice and the consequences of not adhering to them.		
3.	The boundaries and limits of own professional expertise.		
4.	The boundaries of confidentiality, when it is appropriate to disclose confidential information to others and the processes required.		
5.	Measures to safeguard young people and vulnerable adults.		

(Continued)

NOS CLDCD17: Plan and undertake research (Continued)

	Knowledge and understanding	Do I have this skill? How do I use it?	What do I still need to learn?
6.	The requirements of a research brief.		
7.	How to apply research and analysis within your working context.		
8.	Effective research practice and the techniques, tools and sources available to your working context.		
9.	How research data is used by organisations.		
10.	How to evaluate research data for relevance, quality and usefulness.		
11.	Research tools and techniques appropriate to your area of expertise.		
12.	The potential of technology to improve research and how to overcome any limitations it presents.		
13.	How to methodically manage the research process so that sources can be cited and work repeated as required.		
14.	How to evaluate research activities using colleagues' feedback and measurement against outcomes.		

Chapter 3
What makes a good research topic?

What are the bigger reasons (aims) you have for wanting to engage in research? It is likely that you are hoping to contribute to a research agenda for practitioners and seeking to encourage stronger links between the profession and academics or policymakers.

Practitioner-led research may involve reviewing or testing approaches or interventions in practice, or evaluating tools, methods and processes. It may be about bringing in something new or adapting existing ideas. It could be about the further exploration of trends or happenings that are not otherwise being recorded in policy, theory or wider literature.

Above all, practice-informed research is about effective inquiry that leads to progress. At all times, there will be an element of striving to achieve and/or maintain best practice.

Defining career practitioner-led research

Shaw and Lunt defined the key characteristics of practitioner research as follows:

1. direct data collection and management, or reflection on existing data;
2. professionals are substantially involved in setting its aims and outcomes;
3. it has intended practical benefits for professionals, service organisations and/or service users; these hoped-for benefits are often expected to be immediate and 'instrumental';
4. practitioners conduct a substantial proportion of the inquiry;
5. the research focuses on the professionals' own practice and/or that of their immediate peers.[1]

---

[1] Shaw, I., and Lunt, N. (2018). Forms of Practitioner Research. *British Journal of Social Work*, 48, 141–157. doi: 10.1093/bjsw/bcx024

While these definitions were initially applied to the field of social work, it is a sector closely allied to our own, and I think this list gives us a great starting point. Anyone working in the career sector with an urge to conduct research will certainly feel an affinity with this list as a statement of intentions and assertions.

Defining a career research project

Unshackling yourself from what you think are the expectations of any research project is the first step to helping you identify something worth researching. You may already have a burning desire to research something that has bothered you for a while. Alternatively, you might be driven be a desire to enhance the reputation of the sector and contribute to a growing knowledge base, an eager researcher-to-be in search of the right topic.

For practitioners, the overarching distinction may be that a research project could follow one of two approaches:

- Theoretically driven (new ideas developed from reviewing theory and policy);
- A response to what is being seen in practice (measuring and exploring trends).

The distance between practice and research cannot be firmly quantified; it will depend entirely on the topic and intended purpose. To be worthwhile, an inquiry does not have to involve huge numbers of participants or take months of planning and investigation.

For career practitioner-led research:

- There is no minimum or maximum size for any research project.
- There is no firmly, permanently defined audience.
- There is no requirement to directly interview research participants or evaluate practice.

Starting small and close to home

Think about the evaluation of practice that you are already conducting, perhaps on your employer's behalf or on your own, and the skills and tools you use to do so. For example, in your organisation, do you provide feedback or help to review the implementation of policy? If you are a career leader, do you run different types of interventions to see which works best with your pupils? If you are self-employed, how do you market your services to best meet the needs of your client group?

These evaluations are themselves small-scale research projects that are designed to make your practice more effective and efficient and impact future decision-making.

Can you expand upon and develop the learning from small-scale reviews into bigger research projects with wider appeal? Or perhaps you have a gut feeling that while something works OK, it could be better? A completed research study provides evidence of what the practitioner-researcher sees happening around them.

You should always be tentative about what a project may accomplish. When working with partner organisations, you should be wary of giving or being seen to give any promises about what your research can achieve. A project cannot be guaranteed to alter policy, but it may influence practitioners, policy and decision-makers through the right dissemination channels (see Chapter 10).

A lot of career practitioners are inspired by their work or their wider lives. This is often referred to as 'lived experience', where knowledge gained is from first-hand and direct experiences.

What matters most is how the research you conduct can make a difference to career work, to the individuals navigating the complex labour market, their working lives and their wellbeing as they do so, clients and practitioners alike. The landscape is about approaches, evidence, change, continuous improvement, understanding, observation, reflection. It is about building on where we are and thinking about current and future agendas.

Locating your research project

A research project might be:

- conducted in the workplace, during work time (you may even be asked to do it, for example evaluate a specific service or intervention);
- about the workplace, but done in your own time and adhering to workplace protocols;
- independent of the workplace (self-funded or funded by a sponsor who might have a vested interest in your research).

Where will your work be situated? Who will want to refer to it? With so many topics to explore, it is useful to consider what the broad area of interest is for your research project.

What might be the focus (objectives and research questions) of your research?

- Exploring and verifying new approaches;
- Reviewing and re-evaluating models and methods;
- Examining new routes to best practice;
- Producing evidence to back up policy;

- Addressing an issue or problem;
- Investigating and explaining trends;
- Addressing misconceptions;
- Expanding on previous research by extending it into new areas.

Weber et al. (2018) sought to categorise the main focus areas for career guidance and counselling (CGC):

- Career-related challenges experienced by citizens;
- Processes and interventions of CGC;
- Outcomes and effects of CGC interventions;
- Professionalism and competence of career practitioners;
- Organisation of career services;
- Societal context of career services.

You may already have an affinity for working in one or more of these areas. You can read more about the type of research that might fit under each of these categories in their article which is available here:[2] https://www.zora.uzh.ch/id/eprint/143923/1/Chapter_13_European_Research_Agenda.pdf

Potential topic areas

A short and by no means exhaustive list of example topic areas:

- Service delivery.
- Client groups.
- Guidance methods.
- Quality and evaluation measures.
- Equality, diversity and inclusion.
- Local or national trends.
- Labour market demographics.
- Quality of service.
- Practitioner ethics.
- The value of career information advice and guidance.
- Career decision-making models.
- Theoretical critique.
- Models, tools and techniques.

---

2 Weber, P. C., Katsarov, J., Cohen-Scali, V., Mulvey, R., Nota, L., Rossier, J., and Thomsen, R. (2018). European Research Agenda for Career Guidance and Counselling, in V. Cohen-Scali, J. Rossier, and L. Nota (Eds.), *New Perspectives on Career Counseling and Guidance in Europe* (pp. 219–250). Berlin: Springer.

Quality assurance in career guidance

If you are working in the public sector, there is certainly an impetus to engage in evaluation that evidences a robust cost-benefit impact of career guidance. You may be familiar with performance indicators and how they are used to justify and maintain the budget and ensure accountability for the use of public funds against an increasingly stretched financial position.

Quality assurance is likely already on your radar. Considering the principles of quality assurance in the delivery of career guidance might be a possible starting point for a research project.

In their 2019 journal article, Tristram Hooley and Suzanne Rice talk about the different *domains* of quality assurance in career guidance, which they define as:

- Policy.
- Organisation.
- Process.
- People.
- Output or Outcome.
- Consumption.

An open access version of this article is available online if you wish to read it in full.[3]

 **Activity**

We will come back to the Career Development Institute (CDI) research directory later in the book, but for now, you should take a look at it to help you consider what makes a topic of interest in relation to career. You can access the CDI Research Directory via the CDI website.

https://www.thecdi.net/resources/research-directory

---

3 Hooley, T., and Rice, S. (2018). Ensuring Quality in Career Guidance: A Critical Review. *British Journal of Guidance & Counselling* 47, 472–486. doi: 10.1080/03069885.2018.1480012; https://repository.derby.ac.uk/download/f593fd0e53e71121a0298ba6881d0d362f7f7349fb68493d58f7d30f5031ff21/334508/Understandings%20of%20Quality%20in%20Education-pre-publication.pdf

PRACTITIONER QUOTES

'I would like to undertake further research exploring the careers advice, information and guidance neurodivergent pupils are receiving at high school.'

Third Sector Practitioner

'I'm hoping to undertake research in the intersection of careers guidance and positive psychology, specifically around how we can support the growth of hope amongst neurodivergent career planners and job seekers.'

Kath Dunn, Career Consultant

'The last small bit of research I undertook was to look at the labour market for an internal report. I have also looked at the different service usage levels of groups with protected characteristics and at the impact work experience can have on confidence. All my research is in relation to service development.'

HE Career Practitioner

'I focus on social justice topics – always have and want to make a difference to those who experience injustice in society. These themes resonate personally and professionally with me.'

Dr Tania Lyden, Assistant Professor (Higher Education Lecturer)

'To improve the evidence base that supports our practice, and through that support our practice. To generate ideas about how we can do things differently, and provide better support to our clients.'

Dr Rosie Alexander, Researcher

'My research was on the impact of child loss on careers, having experienced the loss of my own child. Having spoken to other bereaved parents I knew that my career confusion was typical. I retrained as a Careers Adviser, following the death of my child, from senior roles in HR. I would have welcomed careers support at the time, and I know many others feel the same. Bereavement and loss are external events that impact people's lives and individual agency in Career decision-making. Career practitioners are generally not equipped for supporting people who are grieving, and particularly those who have experienced a traumatic loss. I believe my research project has been a starting point, and I am still thoughtful about doing more in this space.'

Jillian Millar, Career Guidance Practitioner

'I and the team I manage are all working as research practitioners. We look at what is happening with the cohort of our clients (demographics and survey data), we look at where issues might exist using the data, use labour market information and trends in career decisions stages then we look at activities that can support development. We do this almost without thinking but if we called this research I think we would all have a bit of stage fright. Looking at us doing something outside this we tend to only do this for a reason that benefits the service such as looking at the impact of different interactions on career outcomes for different groups of students. We tie in the research to developments and use the research of others too, to allow us to justify investing in an activity.'

Higher Education Career Practitioner

'My (current) research stems from my personal experience of working as a careers professional in both the English secondary education sector and an English university. I joined a secondary school as their careers facilitator in the year when many schools were expected to adopt the Gatsby Benchmarks to inform their careers provision, and it was a really exciting time to lead that project. When I switched to higher education, I realised that professionals in both sectors had very little knowledge about careers provision outside of their sector, and there is a disconnect between the two.'

Natalie Freeman, Employability Skills Award Manager

The bigger picture

The start of a research project inevitably involves many questions: What will you research? How will you conduct your research? How long will it take? Just as important as these practical questions are those that relate to where your research will conclude.

Can you think of a piece of research that you have read/seen/heard recently that you really enjoyed? What was it? Where did you engage with it? Why did it attract your interest? What do you think was the journey of that piece of research, from its inception through to the point it reached you?

As well as thinking objectively about the topic you plan to investigate, important questions to ask yourself at the outset of a project are:

- What do you hope to achieve by completing this research?
- Who will be interested in your findings?

- Why are you the best-placed person to conduct research into this topic?
- What value do you add as a career professional?

Noting down the answers to these questions at the early planning stages will help to keep you focused, energised and maintain your momentum as you complete your project.

Activity

In a few chapters' time, we will start looking at writing a research proposal and research plan. For now, I want you to make a short, one-page plan that covers the following checklist. You can format this however you like, but if you find it easier to work from a template, one is provided. The example has been completed by a career practitioner-researcher. You can find both the completed example and a blank version of the checklist to fill in with your own answers in the **online resources** that accompany this book. To access, use the QR code or visit the web address at the start of this book.

Checklist: Your early project plan

What's your project idea? If you haven't got a project yet, what's the general area you want to investigate?	While I don't have a current research project underway, I've previously completed research-focused projects within my career that align strongly with practitioner research. One involved exploring accessibility and inclusive design within large-scale public events. Another focused on inclusive communication practices across political and civic institutions. Both projects involved gathering evidence of best practice and producing practical guidance to influence future activity.
Can you get good access to data (existing) or obtain data (new) to investigate?	For both projects, I was able to access a mixture of qualitative and secondary data – including stakeholder interviews, public reports, academic literature and case studies. I combined this with practical insights from frontline practice to build a clear picture of what inclusive practice looks like in real-world settings.
What's your general timeline?	Each project was time-bound with clear deadlines – typically lasting 6–12 weeks from scoping to delivery. This included planning, research, writing, internal review, and producing a final report or toolkit.
Who will be interested in your research project?	The intended audiences included operational teams responsible for implementation, as well as strategic decision-makers seeking to improve accessibility and inclusion. In both cases, findings were intended to shape organisational policy and influence future planning and service delivery.
What support will you need? (e.g. access, time, funding)	Support took the form of clear scoping conversations, access to data and documentation, and regular check-ins with stakeholders to ensure the research was usable and relevant. I also drew on informal peer support to sense-check recommendations.
Is there anyone who can offer you support?	Colleagues with experience in inclusive design, event planning and communications provided helpful insights. I also drew from networks within the wider EDI and career development community to explore different approaches.
What do you hope to achieve by completing this research?	The goal was to influence policy and practice by embedding inclusion in a meaningful and practical way. I wanted to ensure the research didn't just sit on a shelf, but was actively used to shape decisions and improve access for marginalised groups.
Who will be interested in your findings?	Stakeholders responsible for planning and delivery, as well as colleagues in HR, comms and EDI roles. In both cases, findings were shared more widely to inform similar projects and organisational learning.
Why are you the best-placed person to conduct research into this topic?	I combine experience in training, EDI, communications and policy, alongside lived experience of disability. I understand how to turn research into something usable, and how to navigate between strategy and practice. My background in career guidance and organisational change meant I could see the wider context and apply insights thoughtfully.
What value do you add as a career professional?	I bring a practical, person-centred lens to research, rooted in the realities of how people engage with services. I know how to translate evidence into action and how to connect research with real-life barriers and solutions. I also ensure inclusion is woven into the process – not just the outcome.

Chapter 4
Ethics

The practice of a career development professional must be ethical, in line with the values espoused by the sector. By extension, any research undertaken by the practitioner-researcher must also uphold these values. In this chapter, we will start to move from the 'who' into the 'how' of conducting a research project by looking into how, as a career development professional, you can and must uphold rigorous ethical values in research practice.

What is 'ethical research'?

Ultimately, ethical practice is about the continuous attention to the upholding of ethical values and explicit reference to these values when faced with an ethical concern.

Ethical research has integrity. The characteristics could be expanded to describe it as authentic, credible, robust, truthful, rigorous, valuable and legally compliant.

This encompasses much more than a research study achieving ethical approval and the presumption that researchers intend to act ethically. Ethical practice is not a one-off accomplishment and cannot be measured by a researcher's declaration that they 'abide by', 'adhere to' or 'comply with' ethical criteria. However robustly planned a piece of research is, and however keenly an individual is motivated to act ethically, the unexpected can occur.

Beyond compliance

Compliance with legislation is essential when conducting research, as it is in any line of work. There are also specific research protocols you should follow (e.g. the Universities UK Concordat, those of funding councils), and you might also have employer or contractor expectations (e.g. requiring formal ethical approval before you can commence data collection). Many career professionals already feel their work is located within a culture of compliance, and this context may become overwhelming when you first start to consider the parameters of ethical conduct in research.

Alongside fulfilling the research ethics policy requirements of any organisations to which you are linked (if you work in higher education, for example, a rigorous commitment to ethical research will be both expected of and upheld by your institution), there will be expectations of you as an individual.

It may be that you feel you are an 'unaffiliated' researcher if you are not funded by an organisation or part of a bigger research body, such as a university. Remember that you are never on your own and are always representing our sector. The ethical values demonstrated by a researcher impact their own professional reputation and that of any organisation or professional body to which they are affiliated.

You will be expected to comply with legislation, and the practitioner-researcher must also be cognisant of relevant codes of practice. There are many similarities between career sector codes of practice and protocols for research with human participants (in the career sector, it is highly unlikely that practitioner-researchers would be conducting research that looks at anything other than human behaviour).

In your daily practice, it is likely you are already engaged with many of the principles of ethical conduct. In short: you know and do this already; it is just the context that is different (and it is natural to feel initially intimidated by that new context).

Evidencing ethical standards

It is essential to maintain and evidence ethical standards.

Formal ethical review is a common, and usually essential, stage you have to comply with when conducting research within higher education (for example, when working towards a master's dissertation) or when contracted to conduct research using public funds. It offers a level of compliance with expected protocols and regulations and adheres to a structured process. If you are a master's level or doctoral student, your supervisor will support you through the process.

It may be that your research does not require formal ethical review, but you must always follow the key principles that would be required when planning a research project. If you are researching a topic independently, you will still be expected to have upheld rigorous standards throughout your research. You may be asked later on for evidence of ethical compliance. Without this, you may find that dissemination opportunities such as publications or presentations will be limited.

Consider the implications of skipping this important step: What organisation would willingly enable you to share your findings when they are based on data that was obtained without the full agreed consent of participants?

Ethics training

There may be instances where you are expected to have engaged in some level of ethics training prior to submitting an application for ethical review.

Activity

There are some free learning resources available in relation to ethics training. I strongly recommend you take the time to complete the longstanding and well-reviewed free OpenLearn online course, *Becoming an ethical researcher*, as a starting point.

https://www.open.edu/openlearn/education-development/becoming-ethical-researcher/content-section-overview?active-tab=description-tab

Formal (and informal) ethical review

It is most common for formal ethical review to be required when research is being run through a higher education institution (HEI). At the departmental level, there will be a committee, team or named individual with responsibility for overseeing the ethical review process, and members of ethics-trained staff within the department who will conduct the review. The review will be conducted in line with the institution's/organisation's standard ethical protocols, which will comply with and be informed by external ethical protocols.

The stages of the process will be individual to each organisation but will include:

- An application form that integrates specific questions relating to researcher ethics;
- A summary of the purpose of the project (justification, key literature, aims and objectives);
- A summary of the proposed methodology (research question(s), data collection, evaluation, timescale);
- Supplementary materials such as participant information (a participant information sheet, consent forms, debrief information), draft versions of any survey forms or questionnaires to be used and a risk assessment if required.

You will need to wait for approval before you progress on to any data collection (sometimes referred to as 'fieldwork') with participants. You may receive feedback that requires you to revise materials. Ensure you have a clear expectation of how long the process will take and allocate good time for this within your project timeline.

As an independent researcher, you can still evidence the ethical compliance of your project, which may include:

- Producing publicly available documents that evidence your commitment to ethical research, such as a data management plan and ethics statement;
- Including a statement regarding your research ethics in an appendix to any output you produce;
- Engaging with other researchers to obtain peer feedback on your research proposal;
- Partnering with an academic who can run a project through an institutional ethics review as a project partner (this can be particularly helpful if you are aiming for publication in an academic journal; see Chapter 10 for discussion of how to access dissemination opportunities).

I recommend that you draft a statement that summarises the ethical considerations you have made as you plan your research and start working on it as soon as possible. You can then transfer this information into an ethics review template or into other documents as appropriate.

In most instances, once you start to focus on and record your ethical thinking, you will find that it becomes apparent through your research that you have rigorously upheld the key principles.

Key ethical principles

Starting out? Make it easier for yourself!

As a new researcher, it is recommended that you avoid:

- research with vulnerable people;
- research with children;
- research with young people aged 16 and under.

This is because these can be more demanding in terms of achieving formal ethical approval.

Standing up to external scrutiny

Research must be able to stand up to external scrutiny. Specific recording tools may help in this respect, such as creating a publicly available data management plan. Here is an example of a website that enables you to do that:

https://dmponline.dcc.ac.uk/

Legislation overview: Data protection

Data breaches are serious, lead to reputational risk (individual, organisation, sector) and can result in fines. The key principle of all legislation relating to data is simple: data must be treated with respect. You should be clear on what measures you will put in place to ensure data collected as part of your research is managed appropriately.

If you are in the UK, your research must be compliant with the Data Protection Act 2018. This is a UK law that implements the European Union's General Data Protection Regulation (GDPR) and adapts the GDPR rules to fit the UK context, adding specific provisions that may not be covered by the broader regulations. The GDPR sets the core data protection standards, while the Act provides additional UK-specific details on how to apply those standards. If you are outside of the UK, ensure you are familiar with your local legislation.

The UK Data Protection Act states that anyone responsible for using personal data must make sure the information is:

- used fairly, lawfully and transparently;
- used for specified, explicit purposes;
- used in a way that is adequate, relevant and limited to only what is necessary;
- accurate and, where necessary, kept up to date;
- kept for no longer than is necessary;
- handled in a way that ensures appropriate security, including protection against unlawful or unauthorised processing, access, loss, destruction or damage.

You can review the Data Protection Act 2018 in full here: https://www.gov.uk/data-protection

If you are managing a research project, then you are responsible for considering any risks relating to how data is used (collection, storage, processing).

A common pitfall in research is being overambitious and, in turn, collecting more data than you need. I regularly remind first-time researchers I am supervising that over-collection of data is an ethical concern, and this should be something you must bear in mind when planning your project. If there is a chance you will not use the data you plan to collect, then you should not collect it. If your research project appears to be at risk of inadequate completion due to the proposed size of the data collection and analysis within a tight timeframe, an ethics committee is unlikely to approve it.

> **Legislation overview: The Equality Act 2010**
>
> The Equality Act 2010 legally protects people from discrimination in the workplace and in wider society. It is against the law to discriminate against anyone because of their protected characteristics of:
>
> - age;
> - gender reassignment;
> - being married or in a civil partnership;
> - being pregnant or on maternity leave;
> - disability;
> - race including colour, nationality, ethnic or national origin;
> - religion or belief;
> - sex;
> - sexual orientation.
>
> You can review the Equality Act 2010 in full here: https://www.legislation.gov.uk/ukpga/2010/15/contents
>
> Best practices in equality, diversity and inclusion (EDI) are always about going a step further than legal requirements. The Equality Act 2010 or any other equality laws certainly will not prevent every form of inequity and disadvantage. In relation to research, I am unable to think of a scenario where being more inclusive would do anything other than increase the scope and reach of your data collection.
>
> It may be that your topic has an explicit EDI focus, but is important not to be lax about EDI principles in your research, no matter the topic.
>
> If you are in employment, you will be aware that psychological bias has received great attention in recent years, with the focus on unconscious and implicit bias training in professional education and organisational mandatory training. Mandatory training should not be considered to provide a complete foundation for any researcher's training and development. Proactive inclusive practice involves looking way beyond baseline training.

Codes of practice

Your position as a member of the career development profession will shape your upholding of rigorous ethical values in research. If you are a member of one of our professional bodies, you will be aware of the expectations that you agree to abide by in relation to the ethical codes issued to accredited members. These codes take all aspects of practice beyond legal compliance and bring with them a requirement for ethical and moral sensitivity. These ethical codes will also underpin all that you do as a researcher.

Ethical principles can feel abstract and hard to visualise in reality when you are starting out as a researcher. While many organisations and bodies produce detailed guidance on ethical research processes, the codes of practice for the career development sector are also an excellent starting point.

I first wrote about the research relevance of the codes of practice that professional bodies issue to accredited members when I was studying for my PhD. I found them a useful route into understanding the parameters of ethical conduct and now use them to help direct my own ethical reviews of projects.

Let's look at some example codes of ethics to help you see the links between our sector values and your conduct as an ethical researcher. I will be referencing UK codes of practice, but if you are outside of these areas, your own national codes will be similar and can be used as a starting point or template.

The UK Career Development Institute Code of Ethics

In all circumstances members will endeavour to enhance the standing and good name of the career development profession and the career Development Institute
– Career Development Institute Code of Ethics, 2024

The CDI has a 10-point Code of Ethics:

1. Equity, Diversity and Inclusion.
2. Accountability.
3. Autonomy.
4. Confidentiality.
5. Competence and Continuous Professional Development.
6. Duty of Care to Clients.
7. Impartiality.
8. Transparency.
9. Trustworthiness.
10. Fitness to Practise.

In the table overleaf, I have given examples of how the points of the Code might translate into the management of a research project.

Point of the CDI Code of Ethics	Application to practitioner research
Equity, Diversity and Inclusion *Members will actively promote equity and diversity and work towards the removal of barriers to personal achievement resulting from prejudice, stereotyping and discrimination.* *Members will promote access to career development activities and services in a range of ways that are appropriate and ensure inclusion for all.*	All research should comply with the relevant equality legislation to ensure fair treatment of all and promote a fair and more equal society. Equality impact assessment must be undertaken across all processes and should consider an intersectional approach where possible. Research should be designed to recruit from as diverse a group as possible. Researchers should seek to make visible the experiences of under-represented groups. Researchers should be suitably equipped to identify and work with under-represented individuals. Enable practitioners to access the findings of research; research findings should be openly accessible where possible and not held behind subscription-only firewalls. Summary overviews of research with the author's contact details included should be made available in the public domain and promoted to fellow professionals. Dissemination opportunities should be taken up which include in-person sector-specific professional development conferences or online professional training, such as webinars. In acting in the interests of society and exercising integrity, honesty and diligence, the social justice element of career development practice will be evident.
Accountability *Members are accountable for their career development activities and services and will submit themselves to whatever scrutiny is appropriate to their role, including the CDI Discipline and Complaints Procedure.*	There should be a willingness to submit to scrutiny, and an openness to operate within accepted research guidelines. Promote career development professional values in research. The Code of Ethics can be used within fieldwork, to demonstrate the commitment to ethical practice and enhancing visibility of accountability, for example by signposting it within research interviews and participant information sheets. By explicitly presenting oneself as a member of the CDI and upholding the Code of Ethics, the practitioner-researcher furthers the standing and good name of their professional body.
Autonomy *Members will encourage individual autonomy, enabling clients in making decisions in the individual's best interests.*	Fieldwork undertaken should align with core principles of career practice and at no time should the researcher intervene with unsolicited advice or give biased direction.

(Continued)

Ethics

Point of the CDI Code of Ethics	Application to practitioner research
Confidentiality *Members will respect the privacy of individuals. Career development interactions should be conducted in an agreed and suitably private environment. Clients must be informed of the limits of confidentiality and data-sharing at the outset. Disclosure of confidential information should only be made with informed consent or when required by law.*	All research data should be collected in line with the data management legislation. All research participants can expect to have their data and personal information treated with the same confidentiality as would be afforded to them as clients. All research interviews should be undertaken in a suitably private location. Confidential information can only be disclosed when the safety of the participant or the researcher is a risk or when required by law to disclose information conveyed. Researchers must undertake appropriate disclosure, in line with the client group/research participants as appropriate (i.e. basic disclosure, standard disclosure, enhanced disclosure or membership of the Protecting Vulnerable Groups [PVG] Scheme) and to meet the requirements of the Safeguarding Vulnerable Groups Act (2006) when research is conducted with vulnerable adults or young people.
Competence and Continuous Professional Development *Members will maintain their professional competence, knowledge and skills through participation in continuous professional development informed by reflective practice and relevant national standards. Members will also represent their professional competencies, training and experience accurately and function within the boundaries of their training and expertise.*	While a career practitioner may be professionally qualified, that qualification, while it may include research techniques, does not necessarily incorporate researcher skills. Professional development activity may be necessary prior to undertaking research to ensure that fitness to practice as a practitioner-researcher is achieved. Research should not commence until the practitioner-researcher is sufficiently competent in the research skills required for each individual project. Researcher reflexivity and critical self-awareness should be evident, perhaps through a research diary to enable identification of competency issues and professional development needs. The performance criteria and knowledge and understanding expectations of each of the National Occupational Standards for the Career Development Sector can be used to identify professional development needs. Engagement with sector-led researcher training, alongside a willingness to share and train other professionals in researcher tools and techniques.

(Continued)

Point of the CDI Code of Ethics	Application to practitioner research
Duty of Care to Clients *Members have a moral and legal duty of care and will adopt a client-centred approach agreed with the client.*	Role expectations are highly important and must be clarified in all practitioner-researcher interactions. Clarity must always be given at contracting stage to explicitly reiterate the difference between research interviews and change/action orientated career guidance interventions. Cognisance of any employer codes or other affiliations that apply to the individual researcher and regulations relating to the research context. This could include, for example, when working with research participants from another sector (e.g. a university career consultant undertaking research with school pupils). Research findings should focus on client-centred outcomes.
Impartiality *Members will maintain awareness of any limitations on their impartiality, acknowledge potential impact and take a neutral and non-directive approach when working with clients. Where impartiality is not possible, members will declare this to the client promptly.*	Research should be undertaken independently and clarity maintained in relation to the author's affiliated institution(s) and employment(s). If the research is funded, the sponsor should be made explicit and output should not be swayed in the direction of the funders' needs or objectives.
Transparency *Members will agree the purpose and approach to their career development services and activities in an open and transparent manner to gain trust and informed consent.*	An accurate presentation of the work must be made at all times. Participant information and consent documents should be available.
Trustworthiness *Members will act in accordance with the trust placed in them and honour agreements and promises.*	Upon completion of a project, the researcher-practitioner should deliver on all promised outputs. Planning and time management should ensure that research participants receive the same treatment as would be offered to clients in a professional capacity.
Fitness to Practise *Members will embrace reflective practice and maintain their fitness to practise in terms of their personal integrity, physical and mental wellbeing.*	Engagement with practitioner-researcher communities of practice.

Ethics

 PRACTITIONER QUOTES

'As a careers practitioner you are very used to working and thinking ethically, so things like data protection and confidentiality are relatively easy to think about. One of the biggest challenges however is thinking about the boundaries between working as a careers practitioner and a researcher. So, if you are interviewing someone for research purposes, it is important that they understand your role, and do not expect you to provide career guidance. It is also important to watch your internal boundary, and take care not to stray into providing career guidance if you are not in that role.'

Dr Rosie Alexander, Researcher

'I did my research via university study which made the ethics process more straightforward. I had to seek permission from [my] employer to work with clients and finding the correct person to provide permission took some time.'

Third Sector and Independent Practitioner

'I had to work hard to get ethical approval for my research because of the topic. For me it was my own lived experience. I did consider at great length, the emotional impact on me and research participants, and referred to the CDI Code of Ethics to keep me on track.'

Jillian Millar, Career Guidance Practitioner

'Working as an independent consultant I have always had personal indemnity insurance which offers some protection should the ethics of my practice be called into question. I am also registered with the Information Commissioner's Office.'

Michelle Stewart, Independent Careers Consultant

AGCAS: A code of ethics for higher education career professionals

The AGCAS Code of Ethics outlines the values and behaviours required of all members of AGCAS Services when fulfilling their roles, alongside compliance with relevant legislation. It also aims to give internal and external stakeholders confidence and trust in their dealings with the HE careers profession.

– AGCAS Code of Ethics, 2025

>  **Activity**
>
> If you work in higher education in the UK, it is likely that you are a member of AGCAS. I have included an activity at the end of this chapter for you to consider the relevance of the AGCAS Code of Ethics to your specific research project or to career research in general.

Key principles

As professional learning experts in our sector, Claire Johnson and Siobhan Neary have written previously about research as a form of CPD. When discussing the steps towards becoming a practitioner-researcher, they produced a clear list of activity areas to help researchers engage with ethical considerations when conducting a research project.

Focused on human participants in research, they highlighted how the main activities for ethical review for practitioner-researchers involve consideration of the following: informed consent, coercion, incentives, withdrawal, anonymity and confidentiality, risk assessment, debriefing and confirmation. (See: Johnson, C. and Neary, S. (2016) *CPD for the Career Development Professional*, Bath: Trotman.) In the following table, I have given some examples of what these ethical considerations might look like as part of a project to help you visualise research ethics in action.

Activity area	Examples
Informed consent	All research participants are fully informed about the research purpose and the general topic, alongside the position of their participation in the project. Consent is gained from all participants prior to participation. Interview participants are provided with information prior to being interviewed or prior to completing a survey. Where face-to-face interviews take place, a consent form is signed by the researcher following the interview participant's verbal consent. Any participant information form and informed consent form used comply with wider research council guidance on the expectations of research participants. Information on the project is available via a weblink.
Avoid coercion	Research participants are free to participate or not and self-identify their eligibility for voluntary participation. Recruitment for participants is promoted via neutral means and by reputable organisations. Responses are anonymous. If partner organisations or individuals who you contract with in other ways offer research participants you must make it clear that anyone who depends on your or your organisation for services or finance is not being coerced into participation.
Incentives	To encourage participation, incentives are nominal and offered in the form of a randomised draw. Participation in any prize draw is optional. The researcher travels to the participant where possible, but travel incentives are offered for participation if required. Where possible interviews are completed remotely via video conferencing to meet environmental and sustainability priorities.
Withdrawal	Interview participants can refuse to answer qualitative interview questions or withdraw from the research at any time, with assurances that the data obtained about them will be withdrawn from the project and securely and confidentially destroyed. You must identify and mitigate any pressures which could make it difficult for potential participants to refuse to take part in your study. It must be transparent that there it is to no detriment to the participant if they refuse to take part or withdraw, or provide answers that could have a positive or negative impact on their professional relationship with your organisation.

(Continued)

Activity area	Examples
Anonymity and confidentiality	Participants cannot be identified by their involvement unless they explicitly state they are happy to be identifiable due to the nature of their situation.

Compliant data management is upheld throughout the project.

Participant information sheets for the research includes specific information about data use and data rights.

Suitable, confidential venues are used for research interviews.

The researcher does not to share information from one participant with another. |
| Risk assessment | All venues for research interviews are health and safety compliant and publicly located but confidential locations are used for the physical safety of the researcher and participants.

Colleagues are notified when the researcher is undertaking one-to-one research interviews alone.

Care is taken that no psychological harm should come to research participants, specifically in consideration of emotional wellbeing. This covers any harm in relation to possibility that the discussion of personal career decisions and close family background can trigger emotional responses or psychological discomfort.

By using the tools and technique of guidance counselling any potentially emotive topics are appropriately addressed in a participant-centred manner.

If you will be using your workplace or that of another organisation to conduct any fieldwork, you must have the express written permission of a responsible party.

Clear parameters are set that mean research interviews do not take the form of a counselling intervention.

Consideration that vulnerable adults could potentially be amongst survey respondents is taken prior to contacting any individuals identified as potential interview participants, to ensure support is available for the researcher and participant if required.

Ensure good time management, so that ethics are not sacrificed for expediency. |
| Debriefing | The researcher passes on the findings of the research to participants who wish to be kept informed following completion of the project.

Any obligations to funders in relation to summary reports of the work are met. |
| Confirmation | In line with career guidance interviewing techniques, the responses of all participants are clarified during the interviews.

Research participants can be given the opportunity to check the narrative they have given after transcription and summarising. |

> **Use your support networks!**
>
> You are now part of a career research and knowledge community, as well as your existing networks and communities of practice. It is vital that as a practitioner-researcher you are well supported to deal with an ethical challenge when one arises.
>
> - Who might be able to review your research proposal?
> - Who might offer robust and meaningful peer feedback on your research?
> - Who can you turn to if your research becomes challenging?

Mitigating and responding to challenges of impartiality

There may be times when you feel your impartiality as a researcher could be compromised, and it is important to acknowledge this when planning a project. You cannot avoid ethical challenges entirely, and when they arise, you should be prepared to find ways to mitigate any threats.

The Economic and Social Research Council (the UK research council that I feel is most closely aligned with the type of research conducted within our sector) has six key principles for ethical research, which are as follows:

- Research should aim to maximise benefit for individuals and society and minimise risk and harm.
- The rights and dignity of individuals and groups should be respected.
- Wherever possible, participation should be voluntary and appropriately informed.
- Research should be conducted with integrity and transparency.
- Lines of responsibility and accountability should be clearly defined.
- Independence of research should be maintained, and where conflicts of interest cannot be avoided, they should be made explicit.

(Economic and Social Research Council, 2021, available at: https://www.ukri.org/councils/esrc/guidance-for-applicants/research-ethics-guidance/framework-for-research-ethics/our-core-principles/)

While the majority of the ESRC principles are clear and self-explanatory, it is worth expanding on the final point. It is possible that your research will be partly, or fully, funded by a sponsor of some sort who has a vested interest in the research findings and may even have proposed the original research project topic area. While the project may change once it becomes 'yours', the organisation may still consider some or all of the output to be their sponsored research. How do you maintain a fully independent stance in this instance? It may be that negotiation and compromise are required: perhaps your funder may like first sight of any research findings and selected outputs prior to publication. Furthermore, in the event that there should be any politically sensitive findings within the research, might elements be subject to embargo for an agreed time period?

It is my experience that all funders and sponsors are generally supportive and keen to discover the outcomes of any research, but it is important to give this aspect due care and attention.

Responding to an ethical challenge

No matter how well planned your research project is, the unexpected can occur, particularly when research participants are given the opportunity to give free-text answers in surveys or to undertake qualitative interviews. It is one thing to complete an ethics proposal and meet expected standards on paper but another to operate ethically in practice; it is in the response one takes to ethical challenges that ethical values can be proven. There will always be times when ethical practice is limited to individual accountability; ultimately, it is how the researcher conducts oneself in all aspects of their research that is important and to be able to take ownership of any decisions taken.

While professionalism and ethical practice are closely linked, the individual must have the capacity to acknowledge a scenario as containing an ethical concern, for which ethics training may be required.

 **Activity**

AGCAS: A code of ethics for higher education career professionals

The AGCAS Code of Ethics (available at: www.agcas.org.uk/agcas-member-code-of-ethics) lists core principles and standards of professional practice for members.

In the following table, can you think of further examples of how the code is relevant to your specific research project or to career research in general? I have added some examples to get you started. You can find both this table and an example of a completed version in the **online resources** that accompany this book. To access, use the QR code or visit the web address at the start of this book.

AGCAS Code of Ethics reproduced with kind permission of AGCAS.

Ethics

ACGAS Code of Ethics	Relevance to ethical research	Can you think of any other examples?
Equity and diversity – design, delivery and promotion of accessible services to meet the needs of all, irrespective of their age, disability, gender identity, race (including colour, nationality and ethnic or national origin), political or religious beliefs and sexual orientation.	Ensuring inclusive recruitment of research participants (e.g. promotion, language, accessible materials). Compliance with equality legislation. Accessibility of output.	
Achievement for all – dealing with each individual fairly and with respect for their life experiences, abilities and potential. To address and challenge inequities where we encounter them.	Role expectations (difference between practitioner and researcher role).	
Impartiality – embedding the principle of impartiality into the design and delivery of career development services so that students and graduates have the freedom to develop their own career paths. Any conflicts of interest will be declared as soon as they are known.	Employer or sponsor expectations and affiliations, prioritising neutrality and independence.	
Confidentiality – the protection of client confidentiality and the right to privacy, acting in accordance with laws that govern the sharing of data, including personal information.	In research it is easy to transpose the term 'client' to 'participant'. Data protection principles. Robust data management. Safeguarding principles (where applicable).	
Integrity – acting with trustworthiness and transparency in the provision of services, the management of expectations and the honouring of promises and arrangements.	Consider research one of many 'services' you are able to offer as a career professional. Do not overpromise. Deliver what you said you would.	
A spirit of commitment through AGCAS to maintain and enhance high standards across the HE careers profession – by fostering good practice across the profession by initiating and contributing to the sharing of knowledge and discussion of professional issues with members of the AGCAS community and adhering to the AGCAS Quality Standard.	Share your findings. Promote your capabilities as a researcher (and in turn those of your colleagues). Engage with communities of practice throughout the research journey. Build capacity in others.	

Chapter 5
Obtaining information and using valid data

You now understand a bit more about the purpose of research and your role as a researcher. In this chapter, we will work through the steps you need to complete to be able to justify a topic through effective evaluation and use of the best types of research to explore it. Engaging with the research of others before commencing your own study is vital. The more critically you review existing research, the more those critical skills will apply to your own work, and the better and more valuable your projects will become.

Using sources of information to justify your project

For any project, you will be required to justify your selected topic. By engaging in some background research, you will develop a wider understanding and broader perspective on your area of interest. You will also come to better understand the type of research that is valued in relation to your themes.

This activity is known as searching or reviewing the literature. The extent to which you will need to write a justification for your topic will vary; it may be that a well-evidenced summary of where your project idea originates from will suffice, or you may need a more comprehensive literature review. If you are required to write an ethics application, you will need certainly need to write a formal summary of your project.

When creating a summary about your project's background, you should assume that your audience has no prior knowledge of your research topic. They do not have anything to go on apart from what you give them. Therefore, the information you convey must be neutral, factual and avoid bias. There should be no hint at the outset that you have already made up your mind about what the research project's findings and outcomes will be. Avoid a one-sided perspective and misrepresenting materials for your own purposes. Most of all, avoid sweeping generalisations and speculation without evidence.

A literature-first approach

When conducting a literature search, it is vital that the sources you consult are of the highest quality. Please refer to the **General resources** section for a comprehensive list of potential sources of robust, career-relevant data and statistics.

Robust sources:

- Book chapters.
- Articles.
- Government reports.
- Surveys.
- Data repositories, for example, lists of publications by research centres.
- Statistics.
- Labour market information.
- Research reports by independent bodies.
- Policies.
- Strategies.
- Minutes of government meetings.
- Conference presentations.

While some of these sources may be behind firewalls or require log-in/membership rights to access, many of these documents are easy to access and in the public domain. They are not entirely free from influence (always think of who the target audience is), but a priority in their authorship will have been accountability. A robust source will generally be identifiable because there will be a clear rationale for its creation and publication, and the content will be free from speculative anecdotes, bias and hyperbole. The more you read, the better you will become at discerning the provenance and value of the literature.

How many sources do you need to refer to? The term 'triangulation' of data refers to the validation of an idea by obtaining multiple credible sources on a topic; when exploring the literature, can you find several sources that agree on a specific point? While looking for validation of a point, you must take care not to ignore conflicting information; consider why there is discord and disagreement and avoid reading only the sources that corroborate your initial thoughts about an issue.

It is highly likely that any topic you research will utilise labour market information. Many research topics may consider the contemporary and changing nature of the labour market: labour market trends, skills utilisation, access to labour markets, the needs of employers, occupational information – the list is endless. As a career professional, knowledge of labour market information is vital in career work.

Be mindful that labour market data is often quantitative in nature and may be presented descriptively to direct you to trends the publishing organisation wants you to focus on. If you believe this to be the case, you might like to seek out the 'raw' data, which refers to the data being in the form it was originally obtained and presented without interpretation. Numerical data is always open to more than one interpretation, so upon examining this raw data, it may be that you spot other trends or areas to explore in greater detail. When looking at labour market information, always consider the size of the data (the sample size) and how far the findings can truly be generalised to the wider population.

Other sources:

- Newspapers.
- Magazines.
- Feature articles.
- Blogs.
- Internet forums.
- Social media.
- Wikipedia.

I am not going to describe these as 'not valid', but they are less robust. This is because these sources are open to bias and inaccuracy and should not be used as main sources of information (unless they are themselves the data being investigated and are being used as an example of misguided information in the public domain!). A more dubious source will generally be identifiable by a lack of evidence relating to research methods and its sources of data, and it is likely to have a hidden, or perhaps overt, agenda. It may even be implausible if you consider the wider implications of what is being proposed.

> ### ☑ Activity
>
> While news stories can be subject to many biases (ethos of the publisher, skewed to the readership), they can be a good starting point as they can give us a general idea of public opinion or issues that require deeper investigation. Open up your browser window and go to the website of any national news media publisher. Look around and see if you can find an article focusing on career, education or employment and adopt a more critical eye.
>
> Can you . . .
>
> - Identify any robust sources mentioned?
> - Identify opinions and unverified statements?
> - Pinpoint some areas for research based on what is covered/not covered in the article?

Exploring sources

Looking at other sources can usefully feed into helping you identify and balance what it is that stakeholders might know, what they want to know and what it is that they really should know.

When searching through the literature, think about the initial questions you will need to answer:

- Why do you want to conduct research on the issue?
- How do you know this is an issue?
- Who is affected?
- What evidence backs your reasoning? (Remember: multiple sources)
- Who else has researched this topic area?
- How much of the story do we already know?

Obtaining the right information is the key to a good literature search. You hopefully find a lot of material that correlates with your project. However, it is very easy to get sidetracked and over-collect interesting sources that do not directly relate to your specific topic. For each interesting source, ask yourself:

- How old is it?
- Who was the intended audience?
- How was data obtained, used and analysed?
- Why might this be relevant to my project?
- Am I certain this is useful now?

Obtaining Information and Using Valid Data

Troubleshooting: Not finding the right information

You know you read or heard something . . . but what was it, where and when?

Remember to use your networks from the start. Work out a short summary of your topic and ask for recommendations for further reading/viewing in your communities of practice or on social media.

Useful tools for literature searching

Google Scholar (https://scholar.google.com/) is an effective starting point to locate relevant published literature across different formats (journals, books, conference papers, doctoral theses and many more). While it will help you to locate some useful sources, you may not always have full access to the text.

Elicit.com is an AI tool to help you swiftly source relevant literature (I will caveat this with a reminder that when using AI to assist your research, you will need to always review for accuracy).

Litmaps.com is another useful site which creates a visual map to help you see how existing literature links together.

Do not be afraid to ask!

There may be times when a journal article or other publication is not easy to access in the public domain. This is where partnership working can be of benefit, and co-authors, particularly those within universities, may be able to obtain access to resources you cannot reach as an independent researcher.

However, if you know of an article and an author and can track them down, there is no harm in contacting them directly to ask for a copy. In most cases, they will be (a) flattered you have looked them up and value their hard work and (b) more than happy to provide the text you need. Who knows, it may even kick-start a useful conversation!

PRACTITIONER QUOTES

'I think collaborating on research as a first step is really useful as you tend to be guided through things by more experienced researchers. Generally people are happy to help and I would recommend reaching out for advice from people who have done research previously for guidance. If you have a question/issue that you feel needs further research then start small and take it from there. Look into the different research approaches and methodologies and then work out which would be most appropriate. Find out if there are any opportunities to share that research with colleagues, or within your institution and you will start to build your confidence.'

Emma Hill, Career Development Consultant

'Being able to really define my area of interest was the first big challenge – unravelling the various ideas and issues floating around in my head, but it was in sitting with a fellow coach that the light-bulb moment came and a way to really articulate my vision. After that, it was really just finding the confidence to take the plunge.'

Victoria Metcalf, PhD Candidate

'The literature review is critical to your study. You need to know what has already been written on your subject, what has been highlighted but what has been missed. You are demonstrating your expertise in the subject area, that you have considered existing research but that you have found a gap which you will now address.'

Emma Lennox, Higher Education Careers Consultant

Chapter 6
Research methods: Quantitative and qualitative data collection tools

Becoming more research-engaged

In this chapter, I will discuss different types of data and how they are collected. As you read, please reflect on your own skills, capabilities and comfort zones relating to the different tools and methods. As well as being comfortable with the different data collection tools, you will also need to think about how you will analyse the data that you collect, which we will cover in detail in Chapter 9. Furthermore, I also encourage you to reflect on how robust data collection methods must evidence a commitment to ethical conduct.

Secondary data research

In some cases, a research project itself can be a fully 'desk-based' review of existing information (i.e. no new data is generated). An examination or re-evaluation of existing data (also known as secondary data) may be a research project in itself.

In these instances, it is even more important to consider the sources of the data you plan to use. Is it in the public domain? If not, will you need to ask permission to use/access it? Will this affect where you can share your findings at a later date? Ethical considerations will still apply, as will a comprehensive data management plan.

Data management

In Chapter 4, we looked at the importance of data management. Let's now look in detail at what robust data management looks like. Consider your whole project as containing data, not just the new data you collect. Any mismanagement of data is time-consuming.

Good housekeeping forms the basis of good data management. In relation to all project data:

- Use clear document-labelling conventions.
- Consider a classification scheme.
- Where necessary, mark your document/folders as confidential and add 'confidential' or 'sensitive' to the document name (if it is inadvertently accessed, this alerts anyone mistakenly accessing it that they should not open it).
- Ensure materials are accessible when you need to access them while maintaining appropriate security levels.

Points specific to electronic data storage:

- Adopt appropriate measures.
- Ensure decryption (passwords, including additional passwords on individual documents).
- Consider the levels of access control (viewing/editing permissions).
- Use additional measures for sensitive data (e.g. relating to protected characteristics).
- Utilise encryption for any mobile storage devices.
- Ensure you have a secure connection if accessing data remotely.

Points specific to physical materials:

- Do not leave anything just 'hanging around'.
- At the end of a project, or once data has been transferred to electronic modes of storage, shred anything identifiable.
- Ensure project materials (and any mobile storage devices) are kept in a locked cupboard.

Remember: These measures extend to anyone collaborating with you on your project.

Data breaches are serious. If any of your data is compromised, it threatens its integrity. While your data may be small scale, think about what the implications would be if any amount of data became accessible and was amended by a third party. Your reputation is at risk; would anyone trust you to run a project again? Might a partner withdraw their support? In a worst-case scenario, you or your organisation could be liable for a fine.

Primary data collection

New data, which you generate yourself, is known as primary data. If you are collecting new data, you need to work out what type of data you want to collect, and why. This will depend on several things, most importantly the topic being explored, but you should also consider:

- the value of different types of data to your audience;
- how you plan to later share and present your findings;
- the type of data you are, at least initially, most comfortable working with/have the skills to interpret.

The last point is often overlooked. You will rightly be excited about collecting your data and engaging with research participants. However, you need to think carefully about what that data will look like when it comes in. Will you need further training, support or might collaboration be necessary to enable you to analyse the data that your research tools produce?

Data types

The two types of data you will encounter and their main differences	
Qualitative data	Quantitative data
• Thoughts, feelings, perceptions • Conveyed verbally or in comprehensive text	• Things you can count (quantifiable) • Numerical data • Results in illustrative statistics
Examples:	Examples:
• Focus groups • Surveys with open text answers • Group interviews • One-to-one interviews	• Surveys
Apart from surveys, these forms of data are usually collected in person, so the researcher must be present for the data to be collected. Qualitative data may be obtained in person or remotely.	The researcher does not generally need to present for these types of data to be collected.

Mixed methods research combines more than one qualitative and quantitative approach. This does not necessarily mean a mix of both main data types; mixed methods could comprise a project completed using two different modes of qualitative data collection.

For your first research project or a small-scale study, my strong advice is to avoid mixed methods research. The best mixed methods projects have a clear and thoroughly justified relationship between the different types and stages of data collection and can be significant in size.

> **Qualitative data collection: A loud warning!**
>
> It is easy to perceive similarities between interviewing for data collection purposes in qualitative research and one-to-one career guidance/career counselling interventions. For example, both the career guidance and research interview or focus group offer a confidential environment in which data is conveyed by the interviewee for interpretation by a skilled interviewer, with clear parameters.
>
> However, career development professionals are not intrinsically good qualitative researchers, even if qualitative research can feel like an easier first step into research.
>
> For many, qualitative research quickly spirals out of control, is time-consuming and lengthy qualitative data collection is arguably best avoided when you are conducting your first research project(s).
>
> When you are starting out, setting a clear distinction/separation of your research from your guidance practice by using explicitly different methods may be beneficial.
>
> **In short: take careful consideration if you plan to conduct qualitative data collection.**

Sample size, targets and response rates

You will often see the term 'sample' used in research. The sample size refers to the number of responses obtained in your data collection. For example, if you conduct five interviews, you have a survey sample of five.

Your target group comprises the people you want to complete your survey: you need to be clear on who they are, and ensure you only collect data from people who meet the parameters you set.

A response rate is the number of people in your target group who participate in full. For many modes of data collection, the less time the participants need to give to participate, the higher the response rate will be.

How many people should you aim for in total for data collection? This is very much dependent on your topic. It is easy to get carried away and hope for the greatest number of responses you can get. This is not always a good idea. In fact, it is sometimes a terrible idea. I have already mentioned over-collection of data as being a poor data practice. At best, you give yourself unnecessary and time-consuming work in transcribing and analysing more responses than you need. At worst, in a bid to obtain as many responses as possible, you can skew your research and invalidate the results, especially if you do not integrate clear screening tools before collecting data from individuals and therefore do not have a clear sense of who has contributed their data.

A small sample that is highly representative is always better than a large, imprecise sample size. Being small, specific and precise in your data collection is a good thing. It enables you to discuss your findings with greater confidence.

When you analyse and discuss the results of your data collection, you can use this precision to your benefit. You have an exact position for your research and, while you will be tentative and exercise caution to avoid generalisations to wider populations that you have not collected data on, the limitations of your project can often be what give you scope to propose your next study.

Activity

When samples go wrong

Review the sample limitations listed below. The first row has been filled out by the author as an example. You can find both a completed example and a blank template to fill in with your own answers in the **online resources** that accompany this book. To access, use the QR code or visit the web address at the start of this book.

Issue	How could the researcher have avoided this issue? What action could now be taken to help mitigate the issue?
I wanted to gain school pupils' perceptions of work in a certain field. I shared a survey with teachers at a school and they shared it with pupils. After I completed my data analysis, I discovered that the teachers only shared it with pupils studying a subject they thought was relevant to the field of work. I do not have the views of the whole school population, just a certain group of pupils. My data suggest that an employment field is far more popular with young people than it is.	*Being clearer when distributing the survey about who they would like to participate.* *They could consider the potential to conduct supplementary data collection with other target group members.*
I was worried I might not get sufficient a sample of responses to my qualitative survey, so I offered a gift voucher prize draw to incentivise the study. Some of the responses were not relevant to the project aims and had clearly been sent in just to enter the prize draw.	

Issue	How could the researcher have avoided this issue? What action could now be taken to help mitigate the issue?
I conducted a focus group but did not record the session, because I had someone assisting me recording data on the day. They wrote up the notes and destroyed the originals as per by data management plan. However, the file has corrupted and I have no record of the data obtained at the focus group.	
I interviewed someone who had been my client previously, and whose background I knew quite a bit about prior to the interview. Therefore, I did not obtain details of their demographic information prior to conducting the interview. I have this information for all of my other participants.	

Data collection: Popular methods

There are many types of data collection tools, some more complex than others. I will introduce the most popular types here, as they are the likely methods you will use in your first research projects.

Interviews

When it comes to qualitative data collection, interviews are probably the most well-known of all the possible methods. Interviews allow researchers to obtain focused, in-depth information from participants. It is likely that as a new researcher, you will conduct many interviews yourself, but you may do so as part of a team or instruct others to conduct interviews for you. What is important is that the data is obtained using a consistent approach.

- Interview data can be collected in written, video and audio format or a combination of methods.
- An interview should take place in a private and confidential location. Be mindful of your personal safety and inform others of the location, date and time of an interview or interviews if you are working alone or when there will be few people nearby.
- You should always aim to record an interview so you can make a transcript and/or revisit it to ensure accuracy, ensuring you use a suitably secure device and storage. All recordings must be deleted once the project is complete. Note-taking during an interview can be distracting for the interviewer and interviewee alike.

- While AI tools and auto transcription are becoming more effective, you still need to check every word that is transcribed, which remains a time-consuming task.
- You should ensure that you have a clear set of questions for your interview that relate directly to your research questions and the project aim and objective(s).
- The interview may be rigidly structured, semi-structured or unstructured (perhaps a misnomer as there will still be some parameters to the interview and the interaction must remain unaffected by researcher bias).

Minimising risk or harm in the interview setting

The interview, possible scenarios:

- Your interviewee may disclose vulnerability unexpectedly during the practice experience.
- Clients may become distressed or upset when discussing sensitive topics.
- You may yourself be triggered by sensitive topics (vicarious trauma).
- Your interviewee may be known to you personally and may disclose sensitive personal information.

The way to reduce or remove risk is to plan ahead and consider possible scenarios and how you will deal with them if they arise. You should act ethically, showing empathy and sensitivity as appropriate. Use your common sense: if your interviewee becomes uncomfortable, you should move the discussion on and not press them for further detail on the aspect that is causing upset. No project is ever important enough to make it OK to cause distress to a participant or to yourself.

Focus groups

Many of the principles discussed already relating to research interviews also stand true for focus groups. You may have been part of a focus group yourself previously, as they are often used in market research (product or service testing). Focus groups are a good way of obtaining data in a shorter amount of time than it would take to conduct individual interviews. The nature of the data that is obtained will be different, however, and will be shaped by interactions between the participants. Focus groups can have clear disadvantages too. Might the participants try to agree with one another out of politeness? Could the most dominant voice take over?

When setting up a focus group, there are certain things to be mindful of:

- Will you have just one core target group, or will there be different focus groups for people who have different background characteristics?
- What sort of prompts or stimuli will you use to start the discussion?
- Will you be both the researcher and the interviewer, or will you ask someone else to lead the session so you can observe?

Incentives

You may be concerned that offering incentives to your research participants has ethical implications. Incentives should be nominal and are offered for a good reason; when approaching research participants, you will be asking people to give up their time for free. Hopefully, people will be interested in participating, but there may be times when offering an incentive to research participants enables a greater response rate.

Incentives usually come in the form of a gift voucher or reimbursement of costs, to show your appreciation and compensate participants for any 'out-of-pocket' expenses.

While much research is now conducted online, there may still be times when you want people to attend in person. When asking people to travel to an interview or focus group, you may want to offer to cover costs such as travel. Good planning will mean you can work out whether it is more economical to travel to your participants rather than them travelling to you.

For focus groups, light refreshments can not only be appreciated but may even encourage participants who do not know one another to warm up to one another informally before the session begins.

Online surveys can also be incentivised, not necessarily with a gift for every participant but perhaps with the offer of entry to a prize draw.

Risk assessment

It is necessary to conduct a risk assessment for some types of research.

A risk assessment involves:

- identifying possible hazards (which can include lone working or discussion of sensitive topics);
- consideration of the likelihood of harm and its seriousness;
- what action you may need to take to minimise or remove the risk altogether;

Risk assessment templates are freely available; if one is required, use a template issued by a health and safety body or your nation's health and safety executive.

Online data collection: Surveys

Surveys and questionnaires can be used to collect both quantitative and qualitative data. It is quite rare now for surveys to be completed in person. Even if you are seeking responses at a live event, it is likely you will offer people the opportunity to complete a survey via a mobile device or draw their attention to a QR code directing them to an online platform. There is an abundance of online tools available for data collection.

If you are conducting research on behalf of your employer, they may have a preferred platform, and perhaps a paid-for account you can access. You must ensure the survey platform you use is compliant with relevant data protection legislation, which can be easily overlooked if, for example, you wish to conduct a survey in one country, but the platform you are using is owned/located in another, with different data protection laws in place.

Some of the more popular survey platforms include:

- SurveyMonkey: https://www.surveymonkey.com/
- Qualtrics: https://www.qualtrics.com/
- QuestionPro: https://www.questionpro.com/
- Survey Hero: https://www.surveyhero.com/

You will, in most cases, need to be able to extract (download) your raw data (survey results). Therefore, any survey platform you use should enable you to do this. This may not be offered with a basic account, and you should factor in whether this additional feature requires a subscription account. Paid-for accounts may have other beneficial or essential features for your data collection, perhaps allowing for a higher number of responses or access to integrated data analysis tools.

You do not have to use a specific survey platform to conduct a survey. Other formats may work as well, such as a Google or Microsoft Form, or a simple written questionnaire shared by email.

Surveys: Key points to remember

- Be aware of length: the shorter, the better.
- The principles of clear and effective communication should be upheld in the survey text; participants must understand what is being asked of them.
- Think carefully about the type of questions you use and whether they will enable you to collect the data you need.

- All questions should be posed neutrally.
- Ensure you use some screening tools: basic demographic information that ensures your survey has been completed by those in your target group.
- Do not include questions that are superfluous to the research.
- It can be helpful to include a final question regarding the user's experience of the questionnaire: were there any answers they might have wished to elaborate on, provide further context on or they felt their answers did not fully reflect their feelings?

Survey design

Surveys are your opportunity to ask questions and obtain answers. It is in the accuracy of both the questions and the way in which answers can be given that makes or breaks a project.

You should give a good amount of thought to the types of questions you want to ask and the type of data they will result in; will you be confident and capable of processing the data that the answers contain?

The main types of responses are:

Fixed responses: Simple yes/no and other responses to closed questions. These can be great for getting background data or ensuring you have the right respondents for your survey.

Flexible responses: Multiple-choice answers may offer further closed options or start to introduce ratings.

Scaling responses: A Likert scale (usually five to seven options) or other numerical preferences.

Open responses: Free-text replies.

Here are some examples of questions that fall into each of these categories:

Fixed/closed questions	Multiple choice	Scale	Open questions
Do you like it when it snows? Yes/No	Which of the following types of weather do you like? Warm Cold Snow Rain Windy Mild Freezing	Put the following seasons in your order of preference, from 1–4 (with 1 being your preferred season and 4 being your least preferred season) Spring Summer Autumn Winter	What do you like about the season of spring?
Are you a career adviser who runs a private practice? Yes/No	What age client group do you work with? 0–11 12–15 16–18 19–30 31–55 55+	On a scale of 1–5 how comfortable are you working with clients who are post-retirement? 1 uncomfortable 2 slightly uncomfortable 3 neutral 4 fairly comfortable 5 comfortable	The topics I would expect to arise in a post-retirement career conversation are . . .

Pilot surveys

It is always sensible to test out a survey before it goes live (and the same applies to research interviews). If appropriate, have a list of questions ready for your trial users and invite questions from them to help streamline and avoid any possible glitches.

Possible questions to ask survey testers:

- Was the question order logical?
- Was there anything else they would have liked to have been able to mention?
- Did they feel any key data were not asked for?
- Were there any technical terms or jargon that they did not understand?
- Did you understand why you were being asked for this information?
- Were they comfortable sharing their answers?
- Did they feel they were being encouraged to give a certain answer at any point?
- Do you know how your data will be used?
- Did you have any technical challenges?

The number of trial users you target will depend on the project and the intended sample size you hope to obtain. If you are aiming for a significant amount of quantitative data, it will also be prudent to conduct some preliminary testing of the data, after which you may wish to refine the questions.

Planning for inclusive data collection

All research should be designed to recruit as representative (and therefore diverse) a sample of participants as possible. Accessible research requires a commitment to inclusion at every stage. Equality impact assessment of processes involved in the research should be undertaken, where required, in relation to specific diversity groups.

It is difficult to be prescriptive, but here are some broad suggestions regarding how inclusive approaches to data collection might look in practice:

- **Language:** Use of clear, direct and inclusive language. Seek advice and guidance on how to use contemporary best-practice wording from equality organisations where applicable to ensure the language you use is appropriate.
- **Format:** Adaptable/flexible and alternative formats (this is more than just font style and size, although that is a good place to start) and the avoidance of overly decorative styling.
- **Reasonable adjustments:** Offering potential research participants the opportunity to request reasonable adjustments so you can create the appropriate circumstances for any interviews and, most importantly, being prepared to make these adjustments.
- **Promotion:** Consider the methods proposed for data collection and how these relate to your target group. For example, will they be able to get digital access to your online survey?

Principles of inclusive design for data collection

Screen readers

In an increasingly digital-first world, an important consideration is participants who use screen reading software and other assistive technology; all of these points will enable effective use of assistive technology. Installing a screen reader yourself can help you better understand the challenges that poor formatting can lead to. A number of them are freely available (you may even already have one installed on your device).

It is likely that the software you use will have some built-in accessibility checking tools, but these should be viewed as checkers rather than 'catch-all' solutions and certainly cannot override accessible design principles.

Focus on clear language use and avoid technical terms and jargon using guidance from organisations such as the Plain English Campaign: https://www.plainenglish.co.uk/

Proofread closely and use concise sentences and punctuation.

Punctuation is important and enables clarity and signposting of sections.

Formatting: left-align documents, avoid centred or justified alignment.

Use bullet points where appropriate, but not excessively.

Use whitespace liberally.

Strong contrast between text and background is essential, and consider, if you do use colour, how any document will appear when printed in greyscale.

If you include images or illustrations, ensure you include an 'ALT' (alternative) text description.

It is becoming more common to use a short video clip to promote your research – if you do this, include a transcript.

Font matters

- Avoid italics, underlining and uppercase text.
- Use non-serif fonts (for example, Arial).
- When converting to PDF format, ensure your source document is fully accessible first. Remember that an alternative version should also still be available.

Depending on the format, the advised font size will differ. For Word documents, use a 12-point minimum, ideally 14, and for PowerPoint use a 24-point minimum.

Remember to return to these principles when sharing the results of your project.

Participant information and informed consent

All research participants should be fully informed about why their contribution is required, given a summary of the research topic, what their data will be used for and how it will be used and stored. They should agree to this, known as giving informed consent.

Participants should also understand that they can refuse to answer any questions or withdraw from the research at any time, with assurances that the data obtained about them can also be withdrawn if they wish, and securely and confidentially destroyed.

In most research projects, it should not be possible to identify a research participant unless they explicitly state they are happy to be identifiable due to the nature of their situation (e.g. refer to them as 'Interviewee A' or similar).

In any supporting documentation, you may want to list details of any funders or other project partners and include their logos, if you have authorisation to do so, as it may help build confidence in your project's authenticity.

If you are conducting qualitative interviews, it can be useful to get participants to complete a consent form in advance of the interview (e.g. via an online form or by email).

Templates for both a **participant information document** and a **participant informed consent form** can be found in the **Project templates** section at the end of this book.

Chapter 7
Writing a research proposal/plan

At the end of Chapter 3, I asked you to think about a research idea. Without realising it, you have probably already got a lot of ideas noted down that will eventually find their way, in some form, into a detailed plan or proposal for your first research project. You are hopefully feeling ready to formalise how your project will progress from idea to conclusion. To achieve this, we will work towards producing a detailed project plan.

Plans and proposals

A research proposal is a selling document of sorts. A proposal is written to convince others that you are capable of conducting a specific research project. It may be necessary to obtain funding or workplace support, or form part of a formal ethical review process.

A research plan is your own record, planning document and schedule for your research. It may even be a live or working document that you amend as you conduct your project.

Some elements, however, will make it into both types of documents. The purpose of both formats is to present a clear overview of your intended research project.

Aims, objectives and research questions

Every project will have an aim, an objective or objectives and research questions to be answered. Draft versions can suffice at the planning stage and will be confirmed once your project is underway.

Your *aim* is an overarching statement about what you expect to do: state what will be happening. In writing your aim, you must take responsibility. Indicate that as a researcher, you have belief in your ability to convey information accurately and effectively. While being ambitious, you should also be realistic: you probably are not going to fix a major problem, so do not claim or suggest you will.

You should describe your aim using solid terms that are both broad and descriptive.

Examples of useful descriptors you might use to present aims are: apply, collect, construct, classify, develop, devise, establish, evaluate, examine, explore, investigate, identify, measure, produce, provide, revise, select, synthesise.

Your aim might also become the working title of your project.

When writing your *objective(s)*, state the goals for your project. What is it that you actually do? The SMART acronym is useful here; ensure your objectives are:

*S*pecific;
*M*easurable;
*A*chievable;
*R*ealistic;
*T*imed.

Your *research question(s)* will take many forms, and it is impossible to be prescriptive here. Once again, you should be specific. The questions should naturally relate to the type of data you will collect. Avoid anything that is too general, and for qualitative research especially, avoid questions that lend themselves to an immediate yes or no answer (e.g. 'Is career guidance a good idea?'). It is likely you will not write your research questions until after you have drafted your justification for the research.

Justification and purpose

The best way to justify your research is by referring to a range of sources that validate the aims of your project. Can you back up your aim and objectives with references to existing publications?

Writing an initial justification as part of a project proposal is your first opportunity to convince others that you are the right person to conduct this research.

This is where you need to clearly state the problem your project will address and explain its importance. Why does it matter that you examine this issue now?

In a few hundred words, can you explain what the research is about (introduce it), explain why it is important (justify it) and present the landscape (contextualise it).

Who else is working on topics related to this issue? What have they said? What are you going to do differently?

Is there a clear example you can introduce related to the issue you want to research?

Draft an overview of what will be in the full introductory section, the length and style of which will be shaped by where you eventually promote your research. If you are aiming to bring your work to an academic audience, you must ensure you signpost the key scholars and theories/theorists. If your work is in a policy context, what key policies are you responding to?

Are there any policies/priorities/goals within your organisation/sector/elsewhere that relate directly to your research idea?

You will have a personal idea of why your research project is needed, which will motivate you to completion, but you also need to sell that need to others, especially if you are writing a proposal document. Who will be interested in your topic? Who will care about the findings? Take good time to reflect objectively on the value of your idea and ensure your justification for your research is bolstered by reference to appropriate sources that validate the aim of your project.

Ensure you keep a reference list for all sources that you have referred to.

Methodology

Your methodology covers data management, data collection, data handling and, most importantly, underpinning all of these elements, is where you demonstrate your commitment to robust ethics. This section needs to be detailed and specific.

Be clear about your position in relation to the data collection: ensure that any potential for researcher bias at any stage in the research process is explicitly addressed.

You may want to not only explain your approach but make some notes as to why alternative approaches were dismissed. Can you justify the appropriateness of your quantitative, qualitative or mixed methods?

Remember: when you decide on what type of data you want to collect, an important consideration is how you will write up your project and share it with an audience. This will depend on several things, most importantly the topic being explored, but you should also consider:

- the value of different types of data to your audience;
- the type of data you are, perhaps, most comfortable working with/have the skills to interpret.

You have to be convincing and clear on how you will collect new data. Summarise your proposed design for the data collection component. Are there any specific ethical issues you can foresee? How will you address them?

Indicative timeline

State specific timescales, but be realistic and ensure you build in flexibility and room for adjustment. Research projects are unpredictable.

Preventing a crisis/needs analysis

There are three things your project needs to be: credible, valuable and completed on time. Can you achieve this? What support might you need to get there? Do you need to engage in any further learning or approach anyone for support? Where could things go wrong? Mitigating risks in advance is better than dealing with a crisis mid-project.

Output

The final section of any good research proposal makes a plan for the writing up and dissemination of the project. You will not know exactly where the project will take you, but you should have an idea of what you will eventually do with the research and what form that will take.

For this, you need to consider what your project will look like when it is shared with others. Chapter 10 looks in detail at how and where you might share your research. Take some time to consider this at the planning stage, as it may shape the project. Think bigger: beyond your natural first audience, where might you continue to promote your work as a contribution to practitioner-led research in the career development sector? Your research will be able to find an audience, but it may be wider than you originally think.

Meeting stakeholder expectations

There are some important differences to consider when conducting research that does not yet have a home and working towards the needs of a funder or other stakeholder.

If your research project is supported by your employer or another organisation, then it is likely they have invested resources (time, money) in you completing the project and may give you access to internal data.

Ensure you have clarity from the outset in relation to what they expect back from you.

- They may require a final executive summary or a workplace presentation.
- They may ask for timely updates on the interim report on your project.
- They may embargo you from sharing sensitive data outside of the organisation after the research is completed.

Be sure to reflect upon and integrate consideration of stakeholder expectations when planning your project.

Checklist

Can you answer these questions? If you can, then you are almost ready to get started!

How do you know your idea is worth researching?
- Who or what will benefit from the research?
- Who are your stakeholders?
- What might the bigger contribution be?
  - What might this contribute to our sector?
  - What might the value be to your workplace?
  - What might the value be to clients?
- What is your rationale for undertaking this project?

Why are you the best person to lead this project?
- Is there anyone else who could have done this work?
- Has anyone else researched this topic?
  - How well did they do it?
  - What did they miss out?
- What do you bring?

>  **Activity**
>
> **Project communications**
>
> I have one final practical task for you, before you get started. This related to how you will communicate with stakeholders and research participants.
>
> The way to ensure your target research participants and stakeholders see you as a convincing researcher is by conveying yourself as valid, robust and trustworthy. It is likely that you will use email to contact stakeholders and research participants. Therefore, you should ensure that your email account (and any other online presence you have related to your research project) looks professional and offers reassurance regarding your capabilities.
>
> - Use a reliable email service provider.
> - Include an email signature.
> - You may want to add a logo, photo or other image to your email account.
>
> Your email signature, what to include:
>
> - Essential: your full name, your role, your email address;
> - Optional: the URL of a professional website or a website where more information about the project can be found, and a telephone number.

Writing your proposal

When you are ready to work on your research proposal and/or research plan, a **research project template** you might like to use is available in the **Project templates** section at the end of this book.

PRACTITIONER QUOTES

'The key for me was planning. When you first start you have an idea of what you want to research, and maybe even some thoughts of what you expect to find. Once you start looking at what other people have written about your research area – or not in my case – you can very easily go down a rabbit hole reading all sorts of articles and research which ultimately has no bearing on your research. So give yourself plenty of time for that initial phase, and pause regularly to check that you are staying on track. Also be sure to have breaks. You have a life outside of work and research. Plan time off and also plan when you need to be really precious about your time, particularly when deadlines are approaching. Talk to others and share your thoughts – I found that this helped me to consolidate my thinking and the direction I wanted to take.'

Jillian Millar, Career Guidance Practitioner

'Main thing is to have the backing of whomever you report to so that you can get research time carved out from regular duties. Recommend to search for a "pain point" within the organization which can create some urgency for the research to actually be carried out within the organization. Build good relationships within the organization as well as external actors.'

Helena Landstedt Wennberg, Career Guidance Professional

'It is essential to have a clear research question or hypothesis, and to be able explain the methodology underpinning your research design – what is it I want to know, how can I find out, what method is best – and to be confident that it answers your research question. For example, counting the number of doors will not tell you what colour they are. Similarly, the number of unemployed people will not reveal the cause of unemployment – however, quantitative data is essential to knowing that the "unemployed" exist as a category, prior to investigating the causes, which may require more subjective qualitative data. The research design should also enable the researcher to establish the reliability and the validity of their data. The researcher should be informed by what is known already (i.e. a literature review) and their writing up should be clear and have a logical structure so that the reader can follow their argument even if they do not agree with the interpretation of the findings. Referencing is also an essential skill.'

Michelle Stewart, Independent Careers Consultant

Chapter 8
Conducting and troubleshooting your project

This is a short chapter, as what you should be doing right now is . . . your research! It is not all doom and gloom, but things can go wrong. Usually, the planning stages of your project will have mitigated against issues that could be foreseen, but not everything can be. I am not going to pretend that all research projects run smoothly and effectively, or that every project reaches a perfect conclusion. Over the next pages, I will simply offer some tips to help you stay on track as you complete your research project, and we will hear from some researchers about how they overcame obstacles.

Consider a research project journal

A research diary offers you the scope to log and record everything, or just specific aspects that stand out to you as you complete your project. Try to record more than just the specifics of the work conducted; make a note of the decisions you make, your observations and self-reflections. This will all be useful material to you in the future when you come to evaluate your project. Remember: when writing a diary, maintain the same data protection standards (password-protected, locked drawer) as you would for your wider research materials.

You may revisit a reflective research diary in the future and find it beneficial as you approach a similar project. If you have a hunch that you should change your approach, your diary notes may help you to justify a change of direction. Go easy on yourself at the start: when you are learning as you go, learning from your 'mistakes' (they are very rarely actual catastrophic mistakes!) is part of the process.

When your research meanders (and why that is not a problem!)

Research is about exploration, and you should always, really, end up in a slightly different place to where you suspected you would end up. You will be there or thereabouts, but via an explorative route. There should be some learning and discovery along the way.

Troubleshooting

Sometimes things will go off track. This may or may not be within your control. All good research plans and proposals offer scope for mitigating the predictable, but as any career expert knows, the world around us is, at times, completely unpredictable.

Here are some examples of what can become a challenge or stall your research:

- Lack of time;
- Lack of skills or the need to undertake training before you can conduct your research;
- Personal issues;
- Over-confidence in or over-committing to a project;
- Lack of self-confidence;
- Changes in your working environment;
- Fear of the project going wrong;
- Difficulty in obtaining background data/information to justify your research;
- Difficulty accessing the data you need;
- Losing enthusiasm or interest;
- Struggling to get people to participate in your research.

With each piece of research you conduct, you will become better at predicting and navigating potential challenges. If you have a well-planned piece of research, alternatives will become apparent when your research methods stall.

Keeping to (borrowed) time

As a practitioner-researcher, you will have multiple competing commitments, all pulling you in different directions and eating up your time. Time management is always going to be important when it comes to finding space in an already busy schedule to conduct research.

Your project plan should have a timescale with built-in adaptability. Keep this under review and consider whether any extra time that needs to be spent on a specific stage of the project can be borrowed back later on, rather than skimping on important tasks. Rushing an element of the research or cutting corners for perceived expediency is never a good idea. If you need to scale back a project, then scale it back. The priority for good research is quality.

Support if you are disabled, have a learning difficulty or are neurodivergent

If you have a disability, learning difficulty or neurodivergence that may present a challenge or barrier to you as you conduct your research, then support may be available. If you are a university student, Disabled Students' Allowance may give you access to specialist equipment, non-medical helpers such as a specialist note-taker, or other disability-related support. If you are undertaking research as part of your employment, Access to Work may provide practical and financial support.

 PRACTITIONER QUOTE

'My neurodivergent (AuDHD) brain does slow me down a little at times. Luckily I have been allocated a study coach through DSA and some great software which I think will help to remove some of those barriers.'

Natalie Freeman, Employability Skills Award Manager

Losing confidence

When self-doubt creeps in, remember why you are best placed to conduct your research and the value of you being a practitioner-researcher. Your research is important, and your perspective is valued. You are not in competition with anyone. People want to hear what you have to say. If you need a real pep talk, apply career guidance tools and techniques to your researcher self. Picture your end goal and remember those times when you succeeded before despite a wobbly start.

Support networks: Communities of practice

The best kind of rookie researcher is one who is willing to reach out for support when needed. The career sector is a welcoming, helpful sector by its very nature. Reach out to more experienced researchers for support and use their knowledge and positivity to drive you forwards.

Social media offers access to some communities of practice that may be a valuable support for your research. On LinkedIn, there is the *AGCAS HE Careers Research & Knowledge Community* and the CDI-managed *Career Development Research Community*. On Facebook, the CDI runs the *CDI Career Development Professional Community of Practice*.

For those who are migrating over to the BlueSky platform, I have created a BlueSky starter pack. This is a list of career professionals engaged with, interested in or conducting research that is relevant to career work, who you might like to follow: https://bsky.app/starter-pack/emmabolger.bsky.social/3lklafxkgdr25 (and please message me on the platform if you would like to be added to the list).

Use your networks:

- If your data collection stalls, who might you speak to?
- If you stall (motivation, time, energy), who can you turn to for emotional support?

I think there has been a data breach!

If you think there has been a data breach, do not panic. There is a process you should follow to mitigate the situation. The steps below refer to the UK legislation, so be mindful that if you are based elsewhere, the terms in your own country may differ.

- Firstly, and most importantly, do not attempt to ignore or hide the breach.
- If you work in an organisation that has a data protection officer or breach team, then report it to them immediately as the response is time-sensitive (72 hours from when the breach is discovered).
- Take action to stop the breach from continuing.
- Assess the impact. If it is high volume or puts the data subject at high risk, then you should inform them of the breach and inform the Information Commissioner's Office.
- Attempt to retrieve the breached data (recall emails; if someone has data they should not have access to, request that they delete it and obtain their confirmation that they have deleted it).
- Put measures in place to prevent the breach from recurring.

Don't risk it!

Never prioritise expediency over precision. What seems like an easy option to up your response rates can be misguided: be wary of firing out a call for extra research participants via your personal contacts. It can result in an echo chamber effect, where your own thoughts and feelings receive more attention than opposing viewpoints.

 PRACTITIONER QUOTES

I asked practitioners about a research project where everything did not quite go as planned:

'I probably spent the best part of a day trying to do my Contents table! Who knew page numbering could be so complicated!! About 6 YouTube videos and several cups of coffee later and we got there. Thankfully everything else went as planned. I also had a massive wobble near the end. My wonderful supervisor kept me on track.'

Jillian Millar, Career Guidance Practitioner

'(I) often did not feel I had the time to write up my research and give collected data justice. Never presented it in person or in print.'

Helena Landstedt Wennberg, Career Guidance Professional

'A few years ago I was conducting research across a university to look at best practice in embedding employability. The amount of data that was returned was overwhelming and I had to employ a research assistant to help me review the data and bring out the themes. I could not have completed the task and do my job at the same time.'

Higher Education Career Practitioner

'*I completed research at MSc level alongside support from my employer. It helped provide insight both for me and the employer to improve the service we were providing. Doing it through work was easier to get participants from a client point of view and with partners.'*

Charity Sector Practitioner

'Oh gosh – sourcing participants for my MRes project! There was lots of confusion as to who I had to approach for permission to access students, so that ate up a lot of time when my ethics application was being pinged back and forth. Once I'd secured permission I thought that I'd easily find 10 willing Y1 university students to talk to me. I heard from 5 but 2 cancelled, so I ended up with a sample of 3. I was so worried that it would render my research null and void, but actually I had 3 wonderful conversations that provided me with some rich data that has been used as a pilot for a larger-scale study. In hindsight, however, I would have planned my sampling differently.'

Natalie Freeman, Employability Skills Award Manager

'Research involves stepping back from our day-jobs, and taking time to gather evidence and reflect on it. It can be hard to find the time to do this. Thinking like a researcher also takes practice, and is a little bit different from thinking like a manager or a practitioner.'

Dr Rosie Alexander, Researcher

'Ensuring you stay in role as researcher, not career coach is important and needs vigilance.'

Dr Tania Lyden, Assistant Professor (Higher Education Lecturer)

Chapter 9
Bringing it together: Findings and data analysis

In this chapter, we will look at how to analyse and write up the findings of your research project. We will consider methods of exploring or 'interrogating' the data, that has been collected, and planning for how it may be shared with others.

Presenting your story

When analysing your data, you will want to explore the individual points raised but also the bigger picture the data presents. Whether your data is secondary or primary, qualitative and/or quantitative, your focus should be on finding a story to tell with the data you have obtained.

You may have an idea about where that story will appear next, but the presentation and discussion of your analysis may differ for different audiences and methods of presentation or publication. This means that while you will analyse as much as you can, it may not all move immediately and directly into a specific structure for output. You should present your findings clearly, efficiently and in a format that means you can re-visit and re-present them for future use.

Data analysis

Firstly, and most importantly, I must caveat this section with a disclaimer. This book is an introduction to research, and data analysis is a huge and complex topic. If you are planning to conduct complex data analysis, consulting similarly complex and in-depth reference guides will be of significant benefit. Quantitative analysis, particularly if you do not have a mathematical or statistical background, can be challenging. As before, if you need support with these elements of research, you should seek it from elsewhere: supportive collaborators or engagement in your own additional learning and training as appropriate.

I will offer a high-level summary of key principles relating to data analysis, but I highly recommend you conduct your own self-directed further reading on this topic. Please do not be intimidated by this; my point is that there are many who make this particular aspect of research their specialism and can offer far more guidance than I can here, which will better benefit the specifics of your project.

Qualitative analysis

Thematic analysis is one of the most popular forms of qualitative data analysis. You will develop codes to categorise your findings, which is, not unsurprisingly, known as coding.

The categorisation themes you used will likely be based on your justification for the research project and should link directly to the aim, objectives and research questions. The themes may be based on the questions you used in your interviews, focus groups or surveys, or may emerge from the responses you received (known as emergent coding). Ethics remains a consideration at this stage, and coding labels can be subjective. Perhaps consider whether another researcher looking at your research topic with impartiality would agree with your coding categories, as this may reduce any researcher bias.

It is most likely that your initial projects will take a narrative analysis approach, where you try to link together the stories your research participants have conveyed to you about their experiences. You will be seeking to initially report patterns and then go on to analyse them.

The way you code will be down to your own preferences. When working through significant amounts of texts, using highlighting or other colour coding can be very helpful, or you may like to use a liberal amount of cutting and pasting between documents. Having multiple monitor screens available can be beneficial. It is extremely important that you do not corrupt the data in any way while coding and categorising. For example, if you have conducted interviews, you should ensure you do not misattribute comments to the wrong participant(s).

After you have fully coded your data and begun to summarise and interrogate the findings, you may wish to use pseudonyms to anonymise responses. Be careful not to do this too soon; working through a list of pseudonyms and codenames, and needing to recall what you called each person, is an extra complication. Anonymisation is only needed at the stage when the research is accessed by anyone other than yourself.

Bringing It Together: Findings and Data Analysis

> **Inaccuracy?**
>
> As you read through responses, you might spot what you might consider to be inaccuracies:
>
> - Did the interviewee give what you might consider to be the 'wrong' answer?
> - Did the interviewee give a response that suggests they were trying to 'look good' or 'correct', or maybe did not know the right thing to say or made a mistake?
>
> There is, of course, merit to exploring the reasons behind this! Believing something does not make it true or factual, and with qualitative research, you are always measuring perceptions.

Quantitative analysis

Quantitative findings are often presented using descriptive statistics, which summarise and concisely present numeric data. Descriptive statistics are often presented in a simple table.

> **Key terms**
>
> ***Percentages/proportions***
>
> Instead of just using raw counts, a simple and direct way to compare results is to work with percentages (parts of a whole as fractions of 100) or proportions (parts of a whole as a decimal number between 0 and 1).
>
> It is also possible to use statistical tests to examine if two percentages differ from one another for reasons other than pure chance.
>
> ***Measures of location (averages)***
>
> What does a typical value in our data look like? Averages try to answer this question. Mean? Median? Mode? There are three commonly used ways of calculating an average. The mean is the most common average, but it is a sensitive measure. If there are a few very high or very low numbers in the data set (outliers), the mean may not be a typical value in the dataset. The mode or median may give a more typical measure.
>
> > **Mean**: The mean is the averaging tool you are likely most familiar with.
> > Sum of Values ÷ Number of Values
> > *(For example, a team scored 20 points across five games, so they have a mean score of four points per game.)*

Mode: The mode is the data value that occurs most often in a data set. This is the most common or most popular answer. There may be two values which occur with the greatest frequency (bimodal) or several values (multimodal). The mode is more resistant to outliers; extreme values have less influence on this kind of average. We can take the mode of categorical as well as numeric data.
(For example, the team scored three points in three games, seven in points one game and four points in one game, so the mode is three).

Median: The median is the very midpoint of the ordered data and is useful if you have outliers in the data. To find the median, you arrange the values in order and choose the middle value (if there is an odd number of data points) or the mean of the two middle values (if there is an even number of data points).
(For example, the team scored three points in three games, seven in points one game and four points in one game, so the median is three).

Quartiles

While the median represents the halfway point of the ordered data, the lower (or first) quartile is the point at the first quarter, and the upper (or third) quartile is the point at the third quarter. Quartiles denote the data points where the ordered data breaks into four equal-sized pieces. Quintiles, deciles and percentiles operate similarly, dividing the ordered data up into five, ten or one hundred parts respectively.

Minimum and maximum

The smallest and largest values in the ordered data.

Measures of spread

Standard Deviation (SD)/Variance: The standard deviation is a measure of the spread of the data around the mean, or how much variability the data contain. The standard deviation is measured in the same units as the data. The standard deviation is the square root of the variance. This means the variance is measured in the original units squared.

Range: This refers to the entire spread of the data distribution and is the difference between the maximum and the minimum.

Interquartile range: The distance between the lower and upper quartiles. This gives an idea of how spread out the data are without being influenced by a single extremely low or high value (unlike the range).

> **Five-figure summary**
>
> The five-figure summary is a concise summary of numeric data. It includes the minimum, lower quartile, median, upper quartile and maximum values.
>
> **Skewness**
>
> A measure of how symmetric the distribution of our data is. Right (or positive) skew data has low values compacted together, and larger values more spread out from one another. Left (or negative) skew data is the opposite.

Data visualisation

Visualisation of data is also important. Especially when working with secondary data, we are not in control of how it was collected, so we may need to explore its distribution and structure before moving on to more formal analysis.

Some ways to visualise quantitative data include:

- Bar chart:
  - Used for representing categorical data. Each bar represents the count of observations in a particular category. Sometimes we might use bar charts for numeric data which can only take a few possible values.
- Histogram:
  - Used to visualise the distribution of numeric data. The histogram looks like a squashed bar chart, but each bar is a 'bin' representing the count of observations in a particular range of values.
- Boxplot:
  - Another way of visualising the shape of numeric data. The boxplot shows the minimum, lower quartile, median, upper quartile and maximum values at a glance, and gives an idea of their relative positions.
- Line chart:
  - Typically used to chart the change in the value of a numeric variable over time.
- Pie chart:
  - Often used in more informal settings, a pie chart typically visualises relative percentages. Bar charts are usually preferred since it is easier to visually compare the heights of bars than the areas of pie segments.
- Scatterplot:
  - A scatterplot allows us to examine the relationship between two numeric variables. Sometimes a 'line of best fit' is superimposed on the plot to summarise the relationship.

Hypothesis testing

Hypothesis testing is where quantitative data analysis becomes really interesting. This approach allows us to quantify the evidence our data provides to support our research questions. We begin by setting out a null hypothesis: some assumption related to our question of interest. Then hypothesis testing allows us to see whether our data support or challenge this assumption, and if so, whether this is simply due to chance or the result of some genuine underlying association or relationship. When carried out correctly, hypothesis testing allows us to make inferences about the wider population of interest from which we have but a sample of data.

There are two main ways to develop a hypothesis for testing:

- A *deductive* hypothesis is likely to relate directly to your research questions and will have been formulated in advance of primary data collection.
- An *inductive* hypothesis will develop once you have taken a summary review of the primary data you have obtained.

Assumptions

The exact form that hypothesis testing, or any other statistical analysis, takes will be determined by your research question and the context of your data. Different approaches are valid for different data scenarios.

Most quantitative analysis makes some *assumptions* about the structure of our data. Do we have categorical or numeric data? How are our data distributed? Are the different data points in our sample independent of one another? Are the variances of different groups in our data similar? It's impossible to provide an exhaustive account here of how different data contexts shape our analysis since there are so many possibilities.

One of the major aspects of quantitative research is examining the literature to ensure the type of analysis we carry out is suitable for the data we have and the research questions we want to answer. Because of this, when using primary data, it is very important to set out how we plan to analyse our data before we begin to collect it!

Software

Many different software packages are available for carrying out quantitative analysis. Some are commercial products, while others are open-source and free to use.

Simple analyses can often be performed in spreadsheet software such as Microsoft Excel or Google Sheets. There are also dedicated statistical packages which often have the option of user-friendly point-and-click graphical interfaces. Examples include commercial products like SPSS and Minitab. Programming-based software such as R or Python is very flexible and open-source but has more of a learning curve since some coding skills are required. There are also cloud-based options now available which do not require software to be installed on your own computer.

 PRACTITIONER QUOTES

'I remember for me a big issue was what to do with my data! I had data from different cycles of my research i.e., interviews and questionnaires from conference presentations.'
Dr Liz Dinse, PhD in Career Guidance

'Be honest about your findings and what they could mean, even if they are different to what you expected.'
Jillian Millar, Career Guidance Practitioner

'Data analysis can be overwhelming but it's the point where the thinking really starts and patterns can be uncovered. It's really important to take your time and work through all the data, ensuring assumptions aren't being made.'
Anonymous, HE Careers Consultant

'. . . [on] my understanding and analysis of statistical data. I constantly ask myself "Am I right? Is that what the data is telling me?"'
Michelle Stewart, Independent Careers Consultant

'As a qualitative researcher I've had to defend my analysis more than once, make sure you use a recognised method and detail your process. This is one of the most exciting parts of a project – it can either confirm and support a literature review, completely disagree with widely accepted discourse, or help construct new themes which haven't been considered before. This is where you find your selling point, what have you discovered that makes your research novel and unique, and who needs to know about it!'
Emma Lennox, Higher Education Careers Consultant

Discussing your findings

Once you have analysed your data, you will discuss your findings. When writing up your findings, you can easily start doubting yourself in relation to tone, style and terms. While you may not always need to write for an 'academic' audience, adopting an academic style in the write-up stage of your project will ensure your work is conveyed as robust, accurate and trustworthy.

A brilliant resource to support you with this task is the University of Manchester-hosted Academic Phrasebank, which has been specifically designed to support all writers who need to report on their research work. It is available here: https://www.phrasebank.manchester.ac.uk/

Where to begin? It is time to return to the very start. You should revisit your aim, objective(s) and research questions before you begin to discuss your findings because your findings must respond directly to them.

As the starting point for your discussion, consider the high-level overview: Have you achieved what you set out to do? You will certainly have achieved it to an extent if you have completed your data collection and analysis. You may think you have not fully achieved your objectives, but that is not necessarily a bad thing.

Your discussion may include any or all of the following, depending on the material generated:

- A narrative summary.
- A list of key points.
- Comparative data to demonstrate trends.

You should make tentative but never sweeping judgements. Never assume more than is evidenced, or suggest that what you have found, in your one small project, stands true under every possible set of other conditions. It is but one project with limitations, and overselling and excessive self-importance will be easily spotted and undermine your credibility.

You should signpost particularly interesting results in the descriptive text around the presentation of your findings. You may need to introduce or reintroduce other sources to validate your results. This is not just a summary or repetition of your analysis; it is about interpretation: What do your results mean? What additional knowledge has been obtained through your research? What has been reinforced or validated?

Remember, your new knowledge does not have to be utterly groundbreaking stuff; it is highly unlikely you have discovered anything that is entirely 'new', but more likely that you have extended existing knowledge into a fresh area. What is your 'newness'? Have you conducted research with a distinct target group or in a different context? What is the value of your new perspective and approach? Can you confirm existing patterns within a new area? Has your research led to a complete reversal, and your findings indicate the opposite was true of what you expected to find?

Robust and credible research is always worthwhile. It is unlikely that your one piece of research will bring about an immediate change in a major policy position, the way decisions are made or how things are done, but it can contribute to change processes.

In your discussion, underpinning every sentence should be a sense that you can:

- clearly evidence the potential for your work to bring about change;
- state the contribution your project makes.

You might like to evidence specific, tangible points and make recommendations for action:

- Can you offer any cost versus benefit improvements?
- What would you suggest that could make a specific difference?

You should look forwards, not backwards. The data you collected described one moment in time, which has already passed:

- What further research would complement the work?
- Where next for the research?
- Who could gain from engaging with this research?
- Can you suggest the next steps to build on the research you have conducted?

You should take time to reflect on the project and the journey you have been on.

- Have you confirmed what you expect to find?
- Were your methods appropriate?
- What are the limitations of the study?

However, you also need to prepare for scrutiny. When you present this work, what questions will be asked of you? How would you respond to counterarguments or alternative viewpoints regarding what you have presented? What might those differing perspectives be?

And no matter how many research projects you complete, you should also engage in a final personal evaluation, reflecting on your journey, noting down:

- what worked well;
- what could have gone better;
- what you might change if you did this type of project again.

Executive summary

Writing an executive summary of your project at this point can be really helpful. An executive summary is a concise document that covers key points for an audience and may even read as a pitch or selling document.

Writing one as part of the write-up of your project may help you extract exactly what the unique, novel and most interesting aspects of your research study are. You will then be able to rework and reformulate the content easily when looking at opportunities for dissemination (which we will look at in detail in Chapter 10).

Structure:

- an introductory summary;
- aims, objectives, research questions;
- methods;
- unique approaches;
- key insights;
- recommendations and next steps.

You may want to transfer this into a short (1–5 slides) PowerPoint presentation.

Elevator pitches

Think even smaller. You have done substantial work, but now you may need to sell it in it seconds to hook people in! You never know when the opportunity might arise to do this. Being able to convey a project with ease will give others confidence in your ability as a researcher.

An elevator pitch is a 30-second verbal summary that includes:

- a description of the problem;
- why you are the right person to explore it;
- your approach to exploring it;
- the implications for others.

Bringing It Together: Findings and Data Analysis

There are endless guides to creating a good elevator pitch available online and plenty of videos of people delivering theirs. The length may vary, but 30 seconds is about the average. I suppose in some countries and regions, elevator journeys are shorter or longer than in others!

You might shudder at the thought of this, but practising in front of a mirror or on camera can really help build your confidence. If this absolutely does not feel like something you are comfortable doing just yet, could you instead condense the most high-level key points into just a single 'elevator slide'?

Chapter 10
Dissemination (sharing and promoting your research)

This chapter is about how to get you and your research 'out there', wherever 'there' might be. Before that, however, I want to remind all readers that learning how to do research and conducting a project does not mean a natural inclination follows to want to share it far and wide. In many cases, the process of learning how to conduct research is the most important part of the research journey; it enables you to critique the research of others more effectively and to be reinvigorated to find new sources of knowledge to inform your own practice.

Your research should be designed to find an audience, but it may be wider than you originally thought. If you already have an idea of where you first want to share your research findings, consider whether there is anywhere else it may find a home. In this chapter, I will also encourage you to step out of your comfort zone and think about new routes to share your work.

Who is your audience?

I have hopefully been clear throughout the book that the value of good research should not be measured only by its size, reach and/or potential impact. Any research project has size, potential reach and impact, its core values are its validity and relevance. Research may be suited to an audience in one workplace or may find a home at a global conference, national workshop or in a journal. All routes to sharing your work should be considered equally legitimate.

Dissemination, or how you might go about sharing and spreading information about your research, should have been considered at the planning stage of your research project. You will likely have an idea of who will be your audience, and you may already have a route in mind. The priority is how you will inform others about the new knowledge you have gained from completing your research activity, and to do so in what is the most appropriate way for you to share it and for them to receive it.

You should consider who your stakeholders are and take as broad a perspective as possible. It may be helpful to think of who has the potential, as widely as possible, to benefit from the findings and recommendations of your research.

It is important to ask yourself again at this point, why do you want to share the findings of your research project? Is it because you want to:

- make a difference to everyday practice;
- lobby for change;
- improve career provisions for clients;
- increase others' knowledge of an issue or issues;
- demonstrate the importance of practitioner-led research;
- contribute to the career sector in a new way;
- advocate for the career profession;
- add value to your workplace;
- evidence your credibility as a researcher;
- build upon the research already conducted;

or a combination of all of the above?

It is unlikely you will have only one reason for completing your research project, and that means you may also be considering different audiences to share your research with and using different modes to reach them.

Moving away from the idea of a hierarchy

There is a tendency to look only at 'publishing' research (this is certainly a pressure if you are employed by a university, for example), but as practitioners we need to also consider where our research can be most easily accessed and utilised by fellow practitioners and other stakeholders.

Publishing is, of course, a way to keep your research in the public domain for as long as possible and should be considered alongside other means, but it is not the only route to dissemination available to you.

It is also important to think about what methods of dissemination you are most comfortable with. At first, certain modes may be confidence-building for you as a practitioner who is new to the formal promotion of their own work.

Where do we see career research?

- Workplace presentations.
- Work newsletters.
- Professional publications.
- Presentations to other organisations.
- Websites.
- Team meetings.
- Conferences (presentations, papers, workshops and poster sessions).
- Webinars.
- Continuing Professional Development (CPD) sessions.
- Training events.
- Academic journals.
- Books.
- Reports.
- Social media, including LinkedIn articles.
- News stories.
- The Conversation. https://theconversation.com

I am not going to suggest individual titles or locations at this point. Career research is often cross- and inter-disciplinary, and it is not uncommon for research to be found in a journal or publication that might not immediately 'scream' career. A review of the UK CDI research directory should give you a good idea of where career research finds a home. https://www.thecdi.net/resources/research-directory

A review of the reasons why the CDI has put together this directory may also help you to consider how and where and why you share your research. https://www.thecdi.net/resources/research-directory/about-research-directory

---

A friendly first audience

Sharing the findings of your research with a warm and friendly first audience can be highly beneficial.

- Could you write an article for a workplace newsletter or present to your department or team?
- If you are based in a school, might your research be of interest to the wider school community? Perhaps you could share your findings with parents and carers as part of an open evening.

> Remember: you do not have to share everything at once. It may be that you want to initially share your approach and intentions for the research, or the background justification for your topic.
>
> These informal, supportive environments can be a great way to get feedback on work in progress and enable you to reflect on the kind of questions you might get when later presenting your work to a wider audience. You also get the opportunity to experience the different formats for disseminating your work and discover how best you feel you can convey your findings to stakeholders.

You have done all this research, and now they want to charge you for it?

There is no point in downplaying this. Disseminating your research may cost you, in time or money or both.

If you want to speak at a conference or other event that requires your physical or remote attendance, who is going to fund you to do that (conference fees, travel, accommodation, time out of your paid employment, other expenses)? Increasingly, there are hybrid and online options to present, which help to reduce these costs and improve accessibility.

If you want to see your work in print, for some publications, you need to be a subscriber before your article can be submitted.

Some workplaces may be willing to contribute to any costs if your research or your presentation of your research demonstrates a benefit to them or was conducted as part of your job. If you cannot get the full cost covered, there may be some subsidies available.

It is not all doom and gloom, and you may be asked to present and even be paid for your time as your profile increases, especially if you are leading a training event based on your research. Research, however, is far from a 'get rich quick' scheme.

Presentations: Conferences and symposia

There are conferences and similar events specific to the career sector, which are generally run by member bodies. These are welcoming arenas where you know you will have an audience keen to hear about your topic. If you are a member, you can expect to receive a subsidised conference fee.

Before presenting at a conference yourself, you will certainly benefit from attending one, so you can see other people like yourself taking to the stage, in person or via video conferencing. After a conference or similar event has taken place, there will generally be a repository where the presentations used may be available in digital form and perhaps also as recordings.

Examples of conferences include the CDI's National Research Conference for Careers Practitioners and the CDI annual conference, the International Association for Educational and Vocational Guidance annual conference, The Association of Graduate Careers Advisory Services annual conference.

Pitching your idea

To speak at a conference or event, you will generally need to complete a proposal and/or write an abstract. In your proposal, you should highlight the key features of your research and why they will be of interest to the audience. Keep it succinct; this is not the place to convey everything about your research, but to whet the appetite of the selection committee as to why your research deserves a space in the proceedings. Think carefully about the themes and topics of the conference or event, and ensure your research correlates with them.

It can be nerve-wracking to speak in front of an audience about your own work, but remember that it is *your* research and *you* are best placed to do this!

Producing presentations

When designing a presentation for use in person or online, your first priority is ensuring you know who your audience is, how many people you will be addressing and the length of the presentation. Will there be space at the end for questions? There are many published guides to structuring a presentation and the specific software programs you can use to do so.

The most important part of any presentation is you and the story you tell. If you are using presentation software, remember it is there only as a visual aid, a tool to help you convey the story you want to tell.

There is nothing other than practice that will enable you to best understand your own preferred presentation style, and how you should and can use presentation software to support you, rather than letting yourself be led by it. You must ensure you are comfortable and technically competent when using any software or other audiovisual tools.

When designing a presentation, however, there are always some key principles you need to consider:

- How much background knowledge the audience has (and familiarity with technical terms) and what they are expecting from you.
- How much do you need to convey? It is unlikely that you need to present any project in its entirety at all opportunities.
- Your aim: Are you seeking to educate, inform, persuade or something else?
- After you have completed your presentation, what comes next? What do you and your audience hope to gain from this?

Research posters

It is quite common to see a research poster session at a conference, and it is something you might even want to work on well before you find an opportunity to present one.

A poster does not have to cover every aspect of your research study. You may wish to concentrate on one specific area, such as the reason for your project, your methods or just one aspect of your findings.

There are lots of academic poster templates available online, which you may want to adapt for your own use, or you can create your own using software such as Microsoft PowerPoint or other design programmes.

A few key principles apply when you are designing an academic poster:

- Substance over style: Your poster design theme may be linked to your overall topic; however, you should not go overboard trying to make a poster a design masterpiece. Use a consistent font and a limited colour palette.
- Add variety: Include numbers, bullet points, infographics, graphs and diagrams. Use relevant logos (with permission).
- Use expected headings and sections, such as 'introduction' or 'overview', 'methods', 'findings'. If targeting practitioners, you might want to include a section focusing on implications or learning relevant to practice.
- Reading direction: Think about how a reader's eye will be drawn to your poster; is it clear in which order the sections should be read? If not, consider numbering them.
- Titles: Engage viewers, but do not oversell your poster or claim to be doing more than you are in the space available. A question as a title may draw the reader in to find out what the answer is. A two-part title may also work: the first part acts as a 'hook' and the second conveys more detail about the poster content.

- Proofread with extra vigilance; it is unlikely a spell checker will pick up errors when you are using PowerPoint or other software to design a poster.
- Less is more: Be succinct, be accurate, use keywords that apply to your theme.
- Tell a brief story; you are presenting a narrative, not just reproducing data.
- If you want to encourage engagement with our wider project, include a hyperlink (QR codes work well for this) to where more information can be found.
- Credit any funders and identify any relevant supervisors/ethical reviewer processes followed.
- What is the message you want readers to leave with? Clearly explain the relevance of the information to the audience and identify key points that need to be communicated.
- Any sources quoted or paraphrased in your poster must be included as citations in the usual way, and a reference list included on your poster.
- Test your poster out on a colleague or fellow researcher: Do they have any further questions to ask that are not answered in your poster?
- When presenting your poster, be prepared to answer questions!

Examples of reading order layouts for posters are included in the **Project templates** section at the end of this book.

Seeking publication

If you do wish to see your work in print, you will need to give consideration upfront to how accessible your work will be once it is published. Do you want to be able to direct wider readers to your work once published? This may affect your choice of publication outlet.

Many academic journals now offer fully open access, meaning anyone can read the content online. Other publications, especially professional magazines, require a subscription and log-in.

You may need to hold off on sending in your article until a specific call for submissions aligned with your theme, or a speculative approach may be an option. It can be worthwhile to contact an editor of a professional publication before writing up your article to see if there is a particular angle that they would appreciate you taking in your piece to best meet the theme or topic of a future issue.

Publishing your research means it may reach a wider audience and potentially have an impact on policy and practice. If you are hoping to go on to conduct further research, possibly with some funding or other support to do so, having a track record through publication will also add to your profile and credibility as a researcher.

After gaining some writing experience and working with an editor, you might want to go a step further and consider pitching an idea for a book to a specialist publisher, such as Trotman!

Writing to a set brief

There are specific expectations and submission guidelines for written forms, which you must follow to improve your chances of being selected for publication.

Professional magazines, websites and newsletters will generally be looking for short practice-orientated articles and new insights. This may be your target market if your research project has focused on the skills and models related to the frontline delivery of career guidance work.

If you are writing a report, the guidelines of the publishing organisation should be your priority, although there are also plenty of style guides for report writing available online.

I suggested a few paragraphs back that you should attend a conference, event, webinar or any other in-person dissemination opportunity before presenting at one. The same applies to publishing; you need to research your market.

If you are planning to write for an academic journal, in the first instance it may be beneficial to work in partnership with an established researcher (i.e. a university academic), who can support you through what can be a formulaic and, at time lengthy journey to publication, via peer review (likely that same academic who partnered with you to get your project through an earlier ethics review!).

There are plenty of guides to writing for journals available in print or online; however, some journals may require you to be affiliated to a HEI before they will accept your work (another reason why partnering with an academic may be beneficial), and each will have a prescribed form of referencing that all submissions must abide by. Bear in mind also that a whole article may not be asked or wished for initially; an editor may want an overview (an abstract) of your proposed article before inviting you to submit a full draft in which you cover the key points: a succinct summary of the issue, purpose, research methods and main results.

Dissemination (Sharing and Promoting Your Research)

Increase your chances of publication!

- Journals and other professional publications may seem similar, but each will have a specific specialism.
- Is there a specific themed issue forthcoming? Publications may only take articles under a certain theme at any one time, which means the time simply might not be right for your article – but the flip side is that this can be beneficial if your research project matches up with the theme!
- Look at the research interests of the editors or guest editor; might they be attracted to your topic?
- Do your research methods fit? There is no point writing for a journal that only takes quantitative research when you have conducted your research entirely using qualitative methods.
- Does your research build on or respond to something that was published previously in the publication?

 Activity

Spend some time exploring research publications available in our area of work.

Below is a short list of publications and repositories to get you started; a more comprehensive list is available in the **General resources** section.

AGCAS research

https://www.agcas.org.uk/AGCAS-Research

Phoenix, the AGCAS journal

https://www.agcas.org.uk/phoenix

Prospects Luminate

https://luminate.prospects.ac.uk/

Career Development Institute: Career Matters

https://www.thecdi.net/resources/career-matters-magazine

Career Development Institute Research Directory

https://www.thecdi.net/resources/research-directory

The Journal of the National Institute for Career Education and Counselling

https://www.nicec.org/pages/24-nicec-journal

The British Journal of Guidance and Counselling

https://www.tandfonline.com/journals/cbjg20

(Some academic journal articles can be read without a subscription; look out for the 'Open access' logo.)

 PRACTITIONER QUOTES

'I started by publishing my research in professional magazines and publications, including the AGCAS journal. I also presented my research at practitioner conferences and research conferences including the AGCAS conference. I then started to publish in academic journals and present at academic conferences.'

Dr Rosie Alexander, Researcher

'A recent training experience was delivered by Dr Julia Yates, who presented her Career Coaching Cards. It really brought home to me how valuable it is when someone who is really confident in their craft can make a topic so practical and applicable. All of these models started as research and she presented really well how you take these and apply them in your own scenarios.'

Kath Dunn, Career Consultant

'I did a poster for the CDI Research Practitioner Conference, presented at the CDI Student Conference. I was a finalist for the Bill Law Memorial Award, and I have written an article for NICEC which is due to be published later this year. I found presenting in person a little bit daunting but OK overall. Writing for the Bill Law Award and NICEC has been more challenging – imposter syndrome again I think.'

Jillian Millar, Career Guidance Practitioner

'So far I have started sharing informal reflections on my research in a blog, have presented a workshop at the 2025 CDI Practitioner Researcher Conference and I am delighted to have been shortlisted for the 2025 Bill

Law Memorial Award. I am really enjoying this stage and would love to do more presenting, but I still feel the niggle of my small sample and think I will enjoy disseminating my EdD research more when I get to that stage. My MRes is riddled with my rookie errors!'
                               Natalie Freeman, Employability Skills Award Manager

'I was nervous at first, but ultimately a little disappointed not to have my research challenged and questioned more.'
                    Dr Tania Lyden, Assistant Professor (Higher Education Lecturer)

'In general, the commissioning organisation has arranged for the report to be disseminated. On occasion this has been supported by my presenting the findings. I have also drawn on the research to write articles for publications such as the NICEC journal or Career Matters.'
                               Michelle Stewart, Independent Careers Consultant

Self-publishing: Blogs and writing for LinkedIn

Setting up a personal blog for one piece of research might be overkill. There are many blogs out there languishing dormant that do little to promote their owner's capacity as an active and busy researcher and may, in fact, give off quite the opposite impression.

A blog may be useful for you in documenting the progress of a research project, almost functioning as a research diary, but publishing your entire findings on a personal blog may limit its reach.

Some larger, more active blogs invite guest authors, which can be a good way to share information about a project. Be mindful of not giving away everything too soon; a blog post can be a great way to encourage readers to find out more about your work. It can lead to others commissioning you rather than you approaching them, in terms of perhaps writing up a longer piece or presenting your findings to an audience in some form.

Example blog: Critical approaches to career and career guidance (COCAG)

https://cocag.co.uk/

Similar principles apply to the self-publishing options available via social networking platforms such as LinkedIn. Social media can be highly beneficial to researchers. A short article can be a great way to get your profile 'out there' as a credible researcher but be mindful of length. Once published, or if you have a presentation slot forthcoming, you might also use a short LinkedIn article or a well-written profile post as a hook to draw readers elsewhere, where your full work can be viewed.

Running an online session

A further option may be to host your own dissemination event. So much CPD now takes place online following the major shift to an increasingly online-first and hybrid delivery in the early 2020s. Many free or low-cost platforms exist for you to host a webinar, online seminar or workshop orientated around your research. You may even be able to use your workplace account and have your organisation's support to deliver a session.

If you are thinking of using one of the major online conferencing platforms, ensure you are up to date with the latest features of the software and security measures, particularly around data protection principles as they apply to participants. If you are recording a session, additional data principles will apply, and consent must be obtained from participants if they or their comments will appear on the recording and be viewable after the session.

At all times remember to prioritise accessibility for participants (a simple online search will bring up a wealth of resources you can review to ensure you maintain best practices in relation to access and inclusion in online meetings) and contact participants in advance to ensure their accessibility needs can be met. All platforms will have accessibility features you can utilise, and simple reasonable adjustments can be offered, such as providing copies of slides in advance.

If you are confident working online in this way, you will have a wealth of tools at your disposal that can be used to engage attendees with your research (breakout rooms, polls, discussion/chat, live reactions, quizzes, whiteboards), but remember that each innovative option brings with it the potential for technical failure! This is another example of how having a partner involved with your research can open up opportunities for more streamlined dissemination.

> **Looking good? Some top tips to for when you are presenting your research online**
>
> - Higher camera angles work best (looking down into the camera on a laptop can feel condescending rather than collaborative).
> - Use as good a quality camera as you can obtain (even the most basic of external webcams makes a huge difference, and offers more scope for adjustment), ensure you are not too far away from the screen and address the camera lens, not your screen.
> - Similarly, try to obtain a microphone that can be sited in the right position, rather than relying on in-built microphones.
> - Aim for plenty of light and multiple sources of light to avoid shadows. Light should fall onto your face and not come from behind.
> - Be mindful that blurred and busy backgrounds, while they may look effective (and also a little staged, does a stack of books really convey expert status?), can be distracting.
> - Be wary of distractions and background noise (which can include echoing if you are in an empty room!)

Promotion in an online world

We live in an online world, and a part of promoting yourself as a researcher will, inevitably, involve you having an online presence of some sort. This may be as simple as your research output being published in a repository, and you may be happy to leave it at that, with perhaps an email address made available to anyone wishing to contact you to find out more about your research.

A wider online presence may be required, though, if you really do want to drive traffic towards your research and network with fellow researchers. Social media is a big part of how people find and engage with research.

I am mindful that any social media sites I link to here could become defunct or fall out of favour and date this book terribly. I have recommended two open education resources as an activity that you can work through in your own time if you do want to think about your online presence as a researcher, and how to use specific platforms to help you build your researcher reputation and profile.

You may, of course, not wish to engage with social media at all, but it is useful to think about how people will find you if they see your research and want to find out more or want to contact you to seek your involvement with other research projects. As a senior lecturer leading a programme of professional education in the career sector, one of the first tasks I set my students is to search for themselves online. It is never too early or too late to think about curating the information that appears when someone searches for you.

>  **Activity**
>
> If you are thinking about your online presence, these two OpenLearn courses are a great starting point to work through some of the key points and principles.
>
> The benefits of social media in academia
>
> https://www.open.edu/openlearn/education-development/learning/the-benefits-social-media-academia
>
> Create a Professional Online Presence
>
> https://www.futurelearn.com/courses/create-a-professional-online-presence

Where and how do you want to share your work?

It is important to think about the method you choose to share your work. You should consider whether the form works for you, as much as how it works for the research being shared, and find the place that best balances these needs. The tables below indicate the benefits and challenges of using some of the dissemination methods discussed in this chapter.

Formal and informal presentations

Skills required	Pros	Cons
Presenting. Thinking on the spot.	Chance to make new connections with others interested in your work. Opportunity to discuss research and build upon it. May open up to opportunity to write for a specific publication or collaborate with other practitioner-researchers.	Time bound (unless conference proceedings are shared with attendees/others afterwards). Requires confidence in public speaking. Access may be limited to attendees only.

Professional articles, reports and websites

Skills required	Pros	Cons
Good writing and editing skills. Ability to work with an editor. Requirement to write to a brief or themed issue.	Can be directed towards a specific, interested audience. Opportunity to direct your work exactly to a specific audience.	Reader access may be limited to member/subscriber only.

Self-publishing

Skills required	Pros	Cons
Excellent writing and editing skills. Technical skills in relation to setting up social media or other profiles. Technical skills in running an online session.	Complete control over authorship, access, length and style. Low cost and easy to access by all stakeholders.	Self-published articles may not command as much respect. Need to find other routes to direct readers to your findings. It will be helpful to have a co-host when running an online event as technical issues can occur when running live online sessions, or you may need someone to help monitor a chat function.

Academic journals

Skills required	Pros	Cons
Excellent formal writing and editing skills.	Credibility. May open up the opportunity for collaboration with established researchers. Enables you to seek out exactly the right home for your research.	Journey to publication can take time. Requirement to meet journal's requirements and respond to peer reviewer feedback. Exposing yourself to external scrutiny, critique and potentially, outright rejection.

>  **Activity**
>
> When planning to do something new, it is helpful to complete a 'SWOT' analysis (based on the acronym Strengths, Weaknesses, Opportunities, Threats – although I will use different terms as I always find these headings alone a bit intimidating!).
>
> To help you to reflect on how comfortable and confident you are in sharing your research in one of the suggested forms, here is a template for you to conduct a personal analysis.
>
> Both the template and an example of a completed version can be found in the **online resources** that accompany this book. To access, use the QR code or visit the web address at the start of this book.
>
> Before making a firm choice about where you would like to see your work out in the world, take some time to:
>
> - explore the skills you already have;
> - evaluate what you are confident in doing and feel you can do well;
> - identify the areas you need to work on if you want to do something new;
> - consider the links, networks and support you need to access;
> - reflect on whether there is anything you might need to overcome.
>
> This analysis is about focusing on the skills you have, the confidence they give you to disseminate your work in each form, and how you might address any challenges. I have completed a few rows to give you an idea of how to get started with this task.

Formal and informal presentations

Skills required	Do I have these skills?	How confident am I? What worries me about this method? What do I need to address?	Who can help me? What support do I need?	Summary
Presenting. Thinking on the spot.	I regularly present in front of client groups.	I have dyslexia, and this affects my presentation. Different audience to what I am used to, how do I get past my imposter syndrome?	Could I work with a co-presenter to help me with technical aspects? Would it be ok to have notes and ask for questions to be sent in advance?	I need to gain confidence at this, could I present to smaller groups while I get my confidence up, for example, at work, before presenting at a conference?

Dissemination (Sharing and Promoting Your Research)

Professional articles, reports and websites

Skills required	Do I have these skills?	How confident am I? What worries me about this method? What do I need to address?	Who can help me? What support do I need?	Summary
Good writing and editing skills. Ability to work with an editor. Requirement to write to a brief or themed issue.				

Self-publishing

Skills required	Do I have these skills?	How confident am I? What worries me about this method? What do I need to address?	Who can help me? What support do I need?	Summary
Excellent writing and editing skills. Technical skills in relation to setting up social media or other profiles.				

Academic journals

Skills required	Do I have these skills?	How confident am I? What worries me about this method? What do I need to address?	Who can help me? What support do I need?	Summary
Excellent formal writing and editing skills.				

Chapter 11
Where next? Developing your role as a researcher

Completing your research project(s) and becoming involved in the career research community may have left you keen to do more. If research is for you, and you are interested in combining it with other work in the sector, you might be interested in moving in a more formal researcher role. In this chapter, we will look at what academics and others in employment with a research remit do and how you might move into one of these roles yourself.

Continuous professional development: Formal study in research methods

There are many short courses available focused on different aspects of research methods training. Many are run by universities and independent research centres and have a cost attached. You should look for an accredited course that will issue you a document of completion, as this may be useful when applying for future research funding if you need to evidence your credentials.

FutureLearn, Coursera and other online learning platforms also offer short courses.

You should also review the many free many resources that are available. The National Centre for Research Methods website, for example, has both general and bespoke training resources and is available at: https://www.ncrm.ac.uk/.

PRACTITIONER QUOTES

I asked career practitioner-researchers what had been their standout pieces of professional development or training or to prepare them for research (noting that it might not have been explicitly a 'research' event). Here are their replies:

'I don't think there was any specific training, but I did find the book "Succeeding With Your Master's Dissertation: A Step-by-Step Handbook" by John Biggam particularly helpful.'

Higher Education Career Practitioner

'I have actually been involved in an HE research and ethics panel supporting applications for research activity, though have never been the primary researcher. I have also participated in lots of research evaluation activities, partly as a way of understanding the process.'

Kath Dunn, Career Consultant

'Previous project management experience in terms of planning. And a love of reading. If I had been better organised I would have taken advantage of the research short courses on offer at the university prior to starting (to study for a masters dissertation).'

Jillian Millar, Career Guidance Practitioner

'I had my research question (for doctoral studies) burning away from 2018, but thought that only academic colleagues were able to conduct research. It was the CDI Practitioner Researcher Conference and a great line manager that nudged me in the end.'

Natalie Freeman, Employability Skills Award Manager

Master's level study

You may be keen to study research methods in greater detail, which will usually involve advanced training in qualitative and quantitative methods and the completion of a research project as part of your studies. This is usually offered at the postgraduate master's level, through completion of a named degree of MA (Master of Arts), MSc (Master of Science) or MRes (Master of Research), with programmes often designed to set up students for further study at the doctoral level, or a role as a social researcher. While your topic is of interest when studying through formal qualification routes, it is your understanding and ability to conduct valid, robust research that will also be primarily assessed.

> **Postgraduate studies in career guidance: Masters top up routes**
>
> When you completed your training in the career sector, you may have studied up to the postgraduate diploma level only (this is the level at which the Qualification in Career Development and its predecessor qualifications were awarded). Some universities accredited to offer a full MSc in career development may be able to offer you the option of 'topping up' your diploma to a full master's through further study and the completion of a dissertation, usually of 15,000–17,000 words (postgraduate dissertations can be longer, but this is the usual length in our field). You should contact institutions directly to discuss this option and ascertain the format, study mode and duration of their provision.

 PRACTITIONER QUOTE

'I undertook the top up MSc several years after completing my Postgraduate Diploma in Career Guidance and Development. I felt it was important to have practitioner experience before undertaking the MSc, as it provided a structured opportunity to reflect on and refine my professional practice. I also wanted to ensure the topic would be worthwhile exploring, both for myself and the sector. Lastly it gave me a real sense of achievement when the dissertation was handed in, and I proved that I could indeed be a researcher.'

Higher Education Career Practitioner

Academic roles

Scholarly research into career guidance, career education and career development is often practitioner-led or instigated, and those who become academics tend to move into their roles following time spent in career guidance practice.

What is an academic? It is a good question! For those who have moved from practice into research, there may be a lingering sense of imposter syndrome. I am not immune to this myself! I have always felt awkward introducing myself as an academic and prefer to lean on my job titles and the duties of my roles. I tend to downplay my role and introduce myself to people as 'a lecturer who also does some research', but as others like to remind me (shout out to Dr Emma Hollywood at Skills Development Scotland (SDS), who recently said to me, 'Dr Emma Bolger you *are* an academic!' in what I can only describe as a tone of voice that told me to own it).

An academic is someone who is employed by a university, likely starting out as a lecturer or research assistant, who will have teaching, research or a combination of both included in their job role. Academics doing career research may be explicitly located within career guidance and development programmes (there are usually only a handful of these across any country, as they are fairly small provisions) or more likely will be situated within other broader disciplines (human resources, psychology, education).

If you are already employed in a professional services role within a higher education institution, then you may have some insight into academic roles. If the world of academia feels relatively unknown to you (imagine me adopting my career adviser voice here), then it is time to start speaking with academics. I have mentioned already how there will be times when a professional writing partner may be helpful, for example, an academic based in a HEI or another partner within a national organisation. Speaking with academics about their work or asking someone to explicitly mentor you into higher education will be beneficial.

For most, a permanent or fixed-term academic role with a scholarly remit attached to it comes about after undertaking associate lecturer work, perhaps marking assessments or delivering ad hoc teaching. A guest lecturer or guest speaker slot can be a great way into a university role. Perhaps you could offer to deliver a session to students or academics, based on a research project you have conducted. If you are a doctoral student, there will undoubtedly be opportunities for you to engage with teaching while you are an enrolled student and gain experience relevant to academic roles.

As I write this, in 2025, the higher education sector in the UK is certainly in a visibly precarious state. Institutions are announcing redundancies, restructures and change projects on a weekly basis. What will come in the future will remain competitive, but a close relationship with industry and practice will always be relevant to research-focused institutions. Rigorous and pertinent global academic output will only continue to raise the status of career research and practice.

Doctoral research

Over the last decade, doctoral research relevant to and by career practitioners has seen a significant increase. Doctoral programmes and summer schools specific to the field of career guidance doctoral research have been established and continue to grow in scope and esteem year on year.

Taught courses in career guidance and development or related professional studies constitute a small corner within what is a vast global higher education marketplace. The number of students directly progressing from these taught undergraduate and postgraduate level courses to doctoral study in the discipline is low. However, as career work continues to be academicised, opportunities for doctoral study increase. There are two named types of doctoral awards that apply to our subject area. The most common award is Doctor of Philosophy (PhD), although a Doctor of Education (EdD) programme may also be a possible route.

Routes into career-relevant doctoral research can be via:

- professional practice;
- an academic career in another discipline;
- directly from previous academic study.

Doctoral study is a challenge that brings broad benefits. You will join a worldwide career community in academia, improve your expertise and develop your own career. Academically valid doctoral research for and by practitioners builds a body of best practice, enhances the reputation of the sector and contributes to a growing knowledge base.

Finding and financing a PhD or DEd

Applying for a postgraduate research programme can be a demanding process. As a would-be doctoral candidate, you either identify a valid research area and suitable supervisors or respond to a call for applications to a specific project with supervisors already in place. In both cases, you should seek out experienced supervisors who welcome career practitioner-led research and understand its value.

When applying for an advertised project, you must write a convincing research proposal and application and will likely be interviewed. A common additional criterion for funded doctoral places is that applicants hold a master's degree incorporating research methods training.

Sourcing a call for applications in a research area matching your knowledge and personal interests is not always possible. You may need to identify a research gap and propose your own project. Consider the themes of the work emerging from research centres (such as the International Centre for Guidance Studies at the University of Derby), articles in professional and academic career guidance publications and conference strands. Engage with the work and expertise of your potential supervisor(s) and make contact with them early in the process to discuss a possible research proposal. Research which builds links between policymakers, academics and practitioners will impress. Try to think beyond the work: what could the broad impact of your thesis be? How might you disseminate it to a wide and interested audience?

Most importantly, choose an area in which you can maintain interest and enthusiasm for at least three years (if you are part-time, you will need to double that time scale) and commit to it in terms of time and money. PhD/DEd studies may be offered with funding attached (from research bodies, private sector, institutional) or you may be able to secure employer sponsorship. This can come with requirements beyond 'simply' completing the research project, such as faculty teaching or producing reports for the sponsor organisation. Funding may range from a fees-only bursary to a full scholarship covering fees and living costs. Funding is not easy to obtain, and you may discover you need to self-fund your studies. Even with funding, financial commitments may see you taking on or continuing in paid work or studying on a part-time basis.

Example master's dissertations and doctoral theses are included in the CDI research directory. You can also search for OpenAccess theses at: https://oatd.org/

 PRACTITIONER QUOTE

'I was able to join the EdD classes as a PhD student and they were a huge help in that mind-set and knowledge shift toward research. Not everyone can leave for a PhD but I feel like the EdD option should be something discussed more widely and supported by employers.'

Victoria Metcalf, PhD Candidate

Examples of doctoral research by practitioner-researchers

The UK-awarded doctoral theses below are specific to career information, advice and guidance work and/or have been conducted by individuals working as practitioners alongside completing their doctoral studies.

Alexander, Rosie. (2021) *The impact of island location on students' higher education choices and subsequent career narratives: A case study of the Orkney and Shetland Islands*. PhD Thesis, University of Derby.

Barham, Lyn. (2013). *Talking about careers: Personal and professional constructions of career by careers advisers*. DEd Thesis, University of the West of England.

Bolger, Emma. (2021). *Gendered career decision-making: Occupational segregation in Modern Apprenticeships*. PhD Thesis, Heriot-Watt University.

Bradley, Elizabeth. (2013). *Taken-for-granted assumptions and professionalism in IAG practice*. PhD Thesis, University of Lancaster.

Chant, Anne. (2017). *An exploration of the relationship between personal and career identity in the stories of three women: A counter narrative for career development*. PhD Thesis, Canterbury Christ Church University.

Christie, Fiona. (2018). *Constructing early graduate careers: Navigating uncertainty in transition*. PhD Thesis, University of Lancaster.

Frigerio, Gill. (2023). *How can I develop a framework for 'calling-informed' career development practice for Christian women?* DEd Thesis, University of Warwick.

Neary, Siobhan. (2018)N *Constructing professional identity: The role of postgraduate professional development in asserting the identity of the career practitioner.* DEd Thesis, University of Derby.

Robertson, Peter. (2013). *The impact of career guidance on wellbeing outcomes*. PhD Thesis, Edinburgh Napier University.

Yates, Julia. (2017). *A social identity approach to career development: Possible selves and prototypical occupational identities*. PhD Thesis, University of East London.

The Skills Development Scotland (SDS) – Scottish Graduate School of Social Sciences (SGSSS) PhD partnership: A flagship model for doctoral study

In Scotland, the SDS – Scottish Graduate School of Social Sciences (SGSSS) partnership is undoubtedly the flagship model for enabling practitioners to move into doctoral-level study. Established in 2013 by the SDS research team, the partnership commissions PhD scholarships heavily orientated around professional and practice needs.

> Each year the partnership invites academics to propose a doctoral study project on a specific topic related to skills policy, skills delivery and career information, advice and guidance
>
> The partnership offers a 1+3 model, meaning that applicants who do not already have a postgraduate degree with a research component (usually required for PhD-level study) can complete an MRes over 1 year, prior to commencing their doctoral study for the following 3 years. This greatly expands the potential pool of applicants and has seen a number of doctoral students go through the programme who previously worked as career practitioners.
>
> PhD students are matched with a sponsor within SDS, who will have insight into both policy and practice within the organisation. The PhD students are fully funded through their studies and offered the opportunity to undertake an internship, preparing them for a wide range of research-relevant roles after they complete their doctoral studies.
>
> For more about this partnership, and completed and current projects, go to: https://www.skillsdevelopmentscotland.co.uk/what-we-do/evaluation-and-research/phd-programme

Related roles in research organisations

Following formal education or training in research, you may also consider moving directly into a researcher role in the public (including government agencies) or private sector. If you are skilled in qualitative data collection, working as a social researcher may appeal. Alternatively, if your expertise is in quantitative data collection and analysis, a role as a statistician may be a logical next step. From this, you may progress into a research manager in a public or private sector organisation.

Working in collaboration

Have an idea that needs wider input for it to work? Before approaching an academic or research professional with a project idea, it is important to understand their role and position so you can best evaluate how they can work in partnership with you, and when and how to approach them.

Some key points to consider:

- What will collaboration add?
    - Do you need wider skills to complete the project (perhaps you are keen to engage with quantitative research but are skills in qualitative work)?
    - Will project partners be able to fill in gaps in your knowledge?

- Will your project partners open up access to research participants or other contacts?
- Will working in partnership enhance your credibility on this topic?
- Partnership involvement may not be vital at every stage. Where is the involvement of others of most value?
- Who will take the lead? Why?
- What will change about the output of the research through collaboration?
- Will collaboration result in multiple outputs? Who will do what?

CONCLUDING PRACTITIONER QUOTE

'Doing research as a practitioner is challenging because it takes time, and it involves thinking in ways that we are not necessarily used to as a practitioner. We need time for research, and an openness to finding out new things that we might not expect. When I undertook my first research project I hoped to find some clear answers to dilemmas I experienced in my practice. I found that my research certainly provided me with useful insights and possibilities, but it did not necessarily provide easy solutions in my practice. Although this might seem disappointing in some ways, actually undertaking research provided me with much more than I could ever have imagined. I found my practice was greatly enriched by my research and I gained a depth of insight and knowledge that kept me curious and motivated as a practitioner. Although I started as a practitioner-researcher over 10 years ago, I continue to research the same topic now as a researcher over 10 years later.'

Dr Rosie Alexander, Postdoctoral Research Fellow, Aarhus University

FINAL PRACTITIONER QUOTE

I have one final, and for me the most important, quote I received from a practitioner when writing this book. I hope this becomes true for you too:

'I didn't think I had it in me, or that anyone else would be interested in what I was researching, but I was wrong.'

Jillian Millar, Career Guidance Practitioner

General resources

UK career organisations promoting research

The career organisations below collate, publish, advocate for and promote practitioner-led research. They run conferences, events and have publication opportunities for practitioner-led research.

> **The Career Development Institute (CDI)**
> www.thecdi.net
>
> **The Association of Graduate Careers Advisory Services (AGCAS)**
> www.agcas.org.uk
>
> **National Institute for Career Education and Counselling (NICEC)**
> www.nicec.org

Recommended reading

You will likely want to seek out a specialist publication to help support you with more advanced approaches, or if you are keen to engage further in learning about research methods.

Books

Copies of books by the authors I recommend below as a general starting point should be available used for a reasonable price from booksellers or via an e-book subscription. There are many texts covering the same topics. Please do not limit yourself to those I recommend, but do ensure you always select a book from a reputable publisher. I have listed the most recent edition of each book where I do recommend a text, but in most cases, any edition will be useful to have.

A few names are worth looking out for. **Alan Bryman** is a renowned author in relation to social research methods, and any text authored by him or retrospectively reviewing his work will be a good starting point. **John Creswell** is recommended if you are conducting qualitative research. I personally find **Andy Field** an engaging and accessible author to look out for if you are undertaking statistical analysis.

Alasuutari, P., Bickman, L., and Brannen, J. (eds.) (2008). *The SAGE Handbook of Social Research Methods*. London: SAGE.

Denicolo, P., and Becker, L. (2012). *Developing Research Proposals*. London: SAGE.

Denscombe, M. (2009). *Ground Rules for Social Research: Guidelines for Good Practice*. 2nd ed. Maidenhead: McGraw-Hill.

De Vaus, D. A. (2013). *Surveys in Social Research (Social Research Today)*. 6th ed. Abingdon: Routledge.

Murray, R. (2019). *Writing for Academic Journals*. 4th ed. London: Open University Press.

Wheeldon, J., and Ahlberg, M. (2011). *Visualising Social Science Research: Maps, Methods & Meaning*. London: SAGE.

I also, of course, recommend you review the other career-related books published by Trotman that discuss themes and ideas relating to topics of interest for career practitioner-led research. In particular, Neary, S., and Johnson, C. (2016). *CPD for the Career Development Professional*. London: Trotman contextualises research as a valuable aspect of continuous professional development.

Sources of data (UK)

Statistics

This section includes, but is not limited to, example publishers of statistical data on: labour market information, employment rates, census returns, economics, society, population basics.

Nomis

http://www.nomisweb.co.uk

Nomis is a service provided by the Office for National Statistics (ONS), the UK's largest independent producer of official statistics. On this website, we publish statistics related to population, society and the labour market at national, regional and local levels. These include data from current and previous censuses.

Office for National Statistics (ONS)

https://www.ons.gov.uk/

The ONS collect, analyse and disseminate statistics about the UK's economy, society and population.

Data.gov.uk

https://www.data.gov.uk/

At Data.gov.uk, you find data published by central government, local authorities and public bodies.

UK Data Archive

https://www.data-archive.ac.uk/

The lead partner of the UK Data Service provides researchers with support, training and access to the UK's largest collection of social, economic and population data.

STATISTICS.GOV.SCOT

http://statistics.gov.scot

Managed by the Scottish Government, this site provides official statistics about Scotland from a variety of data producers, for information and re-use.

Labour market statistics (Scottish Government)

https://www.gov.scot/collections/labour-market-statistics/

A directory of statistical publications related to Scotland's labour market organised by subject.

Skills Development Scotland Statistics

https://www.skillsdevelopmentscotland.co.uk/publications-statistics/statistics

Skills Development Scotland is the national skills body supporting the people and businesses of Scotland to develop and apply their skills. Skills Development Scotland collect and analyse data on their programmes and activities. This website contains reports and information that has been made publicly available.

NISRA

https://www.nisra.gov.uk/statistics

The Northern Ireland Statistics and Research Agency provides independent insights on life in Northern Ireland through statistics, analysis, research and registration services.

Welsh Government Statistics and research

https://www.gov.wales/statistics-and-research

Statistics and research is the major independent source for current and historical releases of official statistics and social and economic research on Wales.

Statistics Isle of Man

https://www.gov.im/about-the-government/departments/cabinet-office/statistics-isle-of-man/

Statistics Isle of Man of the Cabinet Office acts as the principal collator and publisher of Government statistics.

Statistics and performance (Jersey)

https://www.gov.je/statisticsperformance/

Statistics Jersey is the central statistical office for Jersey. They have professional and operational independence to produce official statistics relating to the economy, population and society of Jersey.

Facts & Figures (Guernsey)

https://www.gov.gg/data

Statistics for Guernsey, including information on population, employment, unemployment and earnings.

Listen up!

To be thought-provoking and informative sources of information do not have to be written down and read. As you start to engage more with statistics, you may enjoy the BBC radio programme *More or Less*, in which the presenter explores the numbers and statistics used in political debate, the news and everyday life.

https://www.bbc.co.uk/programmes/b006qshd

UK Census data

A national census is undertaken every 10 years in the UK nations to create a picture of all people and households. Questions relate to individuals, their household, their home.

England and Wales
https://www.ons.gov.uk/census

Scotland
https://www.scotlandscensus.gov.uk

Northern Ireland
https://www.nisra.gov.uk/statistics/people-and-communities/census

Research centres and hubs specialising in career, employment or related topics

Warwick Institute for Employment Research
https://warwick.ac.uk/fac/soc/ier

An interdisciplinary research centre covering topics including labour market and skills intelligence, education, training and skills, the future of work, welfare and social inclusion, career guidance, development and transitions, job quality, fair, decent and good work, employment practices, regional and sector analysis.

International Centre for Guidance Studies (ICEGS)

http://www.derby.ac.uk/research/icegs/

ICEGS is an international research centre in career and career guidance. Its research addresses how people develop their careers in complex modern societies and what interventions and approaches can be used to enable people to build successful careers and find their way to the good life.

Education and Employers

https://www.educationandemployers.org/research-main/

Education and Employers undertakes high-quality robust research on education and employer engagement that informs education policy and practice. They also collaborate with other leading research institutions and ensure that research produced by academics around the world is easily accessible to practitioners, employers and policymakers.

Institute for Employment Studies (IES)

https://www.employment-studies.co.uk/

IES research and consult on employment and human resources topics, using a range of approaches to provide insights and support to policymakers and practitioners.

The National Foundation for Educational Research (NFER)

https://www.nfer.ac.uk/

NFER carry out a wide range of research and evaluations to answer key questions about education, in the UK and internationally.

CFE Research

https://cfe.org.uk/

CFE is an independent social research company providing research and evaluation services to government departments, public sector agencies, local authorities, educational institutions and providers, charities.

SQW

https://www.sqw.co.uk

SQW is an independent provider of research, analysis and advice in economic and social development. A particular focus area for research is employment, skills and education.

The Organisation for Economic Co-operation and Development (OECD)

https://www.oecd.org/en.html

The OECD is a forum and knowledge hub for data, analysis and best practices in public policy.

Examples of other sources of data relevant to key career topics

The Office for Students

https://www.officeforstudents.org.uk

Data-driven analysis and essential evidence on key trends and current issues in English higher education.

Scottish Funding Council

https://www.sfc.ac.uk/publications/statistical-publication-schedule/

Official and National Statistics covering Further and Higher Education in Scotland

Luminate

https://luminate.prospects.ac.uk/

Prospects Luminate is the home of data, trends, best practice and thought leadership on careers guidance, early careers recruitment and student and graduate experience.

The Chartered Institute for Professional Development (CIPD) Knowledge Hub

https://www.cipd.co.uk/knowledge

The CIPD Knowledge Hub contains survey findings and guidance on workplace issues.

Non-UK organisations relevant to the career sector

While the resources included in this section have focused on the UK, I do encourage you to look beyond the UK nations when seeking sources of information to review, compare and contrast with. Examples of relevant European and global organisations are as follows.

CEDEFOP

https://www.cedefop.europa.eu/en

A European Union agency focuses on vocational education and training and skills and qualifications policies.

European Association of Career Guidance (EAGC)

https://eacg.eu

International Association for Educational and Vocational Guidance (IAEVG)

https://iaevg.com

International Centre for Career Development and Public Policy (ICCDPP)

https://www.iccdpp.org/

The ICCDPP website hosts a knowledge centre that provides up-to-date information on career guidance policies and systems, drawn from countries and international organisations worldwide.

Project templates

This section contains templates and guidance for the following:

- Research project template.
- Research project template, with guidance and prompts for each section.
- Template for a participant information document.
- An example participant information document.
- Template for a participant informed consent form.
- Template for a survey title page (including informed consent and participant information).
- An example survey title page.
- Poster reading directions.

Research project template

Working title of project	
Aim (50 words)	
Objectives (100 words)	
Research question (25–50 words)	
Justification (500 words)	
Resources (50 words)	
Timeline (50 words)	

(Continued overleaf...)

Working title of project	
Data Collection (including ethics) (300 words)	
Data Analysis (150 words)	
Writing up and dissemination plan (250 words)	
Key sources	
Can you summarise your project in a 30 second description or over 2 short paragraphs?	

Research project template, with guidance and prompts for each section

Working title of project	
Aim (50 words)	An overarching statement. Be broad and descriptive about what you hope your project will achieve.
Objectives (100 words)	Who or what are you going to research? Think SMART targets, with goals which are: Specific, Measurable, Achievable, Realistic, Timed.
Research question (25–50 words)	What specific question are you trying to answer? Starting with one of the following words may help: Why? When? Who? How? Where?
Justification (500 words)	Why is this research project needed? What is the issue? Why are you the best person to lead it? How do you know this is worth researching? What contribution will a better understanding of this issue make? What is your rationale for undertaking this project? Can you back this up with references to existing publications? Are there any policies/priorities/goals within your organisation or sector or elsewhere that relate directly to your research idea? What will be inventive and original about your project (new questions, new methods?)
Resources (50 words)	How will this project be funded? How will the time you spend on it be budgeted? Will there be any additional costs? Are there any implications for the project relating to who is covering the costs?
Timeline (50 words)	Include a clear timeline for the project.
Data Collection (including ethics) (300 words)	What data will you collect? How will you obtain that data? How will you ensure that you do this legally and ethically? How will you ensure the data is handled appropriately? What are the specific dates for the timeline of the project?

(Continued overleaf...)

Working title of project	
Data Analysis (150 words)	How will you investigate the data you obtain? What methods will you use to categorise and make sense of the data?
Writing up and dissemination plan (250 words)	How will you present your analysis of the data? How will you write it up? What will your end "report" look like? How will you structure it? What will you do with the research once it is completed? Who will it be shared with? Who is your audience?
Key sources	List all articles, books, reports or other resources. Aim for variety in the sources you use, as appropriate.
Can you summarise your project in a 30 second description or over 2 short paragraphs?	Record yourself speaking or draft an email to an imaginary stakeholder.

Template for a participant information document

Note: The participant information document could be abridged/adapted to produce an overview of your project to share by other means, to attract participants. The list below covers the key areas and points you should expect to cover.

Title of the research project
Overview of the project • Summarise the project. • Explain to the participant why they have been selected to take part and why their involvement is sought. • Provide a link to a website where more information about the project can be found, if applicable. • Introduce yourself as the lead researcher, stating any relevant credentials that add to your authenticity. • Clearly state your contact details.
Their involvement • Encourage the participant to take time to read the information provided. • Offer the participant space to ask any further questions. • Be clear that participants can withdraw at any point.
The focus of the interview • What the participant can expect to discuss. • What the participant will be asked about. • What the participant may be encouraged to focus on.
Possible benefits of your participation • Think broadly and be positive. • Note any incentives offered.
What are the possible risks of taking part? • Be honest here, as no conversation is without risk.
The interview parameters • State the expected length of the interview/focus group. • State the format and location. • State that it will be recorded and transcribed. • Clarify if any expenses will be reimbursed and how. • Note your willingness to accommodate any additional requirements.
Funder/partners • If there are any research partners, state who they are.
Ethics and data protection • Summarise your data management process. • Explain how the data obtained will be used. • Explain confidentiality and state how their contribution will be anonymised, if required. • State how the data will be stored securely. • State when their stored data will be deleted. • Note any formal ethical approval. • Include named third party contact details (obtain authorisation from someone other than yourself in a reasonable position of authority to be named here).
Show courtesy • Thank your research participant for taking the time to be involved.

An example participant information document

Gender and career decision-making project: Information for interview participants

Overview of the project

You have been invited to take part in a research interview as you are completing or have completed a Modern Apprenticeship, and your apprenticeship is in a framework, sector or role where your gender is under-represented.

Your participation is entirely voluntary, and before you agree to be interviewed, I want you to understand what the research is about and what the interview will involve. The interview is part of my research project, which explores career decision-making, gender and Modern Apprenticeships.

The purpose of the research is to explore the reasons why people undertake apprenticeships in areas in which they are typically under-represented by gender. For example, male apprentices working in early years education or female apprentices working in construction. I am keen to find out about your personal background and the career decisions you have made in the past. This will help me to explore which aspects of personal background have an impact on people following trends relating to their gender.

My name is Emma Bolger, and I will conduct the interview. I am a senior lecturer and researcher in career guidance and development and a qualified careers adviser. My email address is emma@scottishuniversity.ac.uk and you can find out more about my work and research on my website at www.emmabolger.co.uk

Your involvement

Please take the time to read the information in this document carefully. You are free to discuss it with others if you want to. You will be asked to sign a consent form stating you agree to your participation. Please ask me if there is anything that is not clear or if you would like more information. If you decide to take part and then change your mind, you are free to withdraw from the research at any time and I will delete the data you have provided to me.

The focus of the interview

You will be asked some questions about your career history. You will be encouraged to highlight specific key points when you have made career decisions in the past. You may also mention how you plan to make career decisions in the future. You will be asked to complete a short questionnaire to confirm personal details.

Possible benefits of your participation

While this is not a career guidance interview, you might find the interview helps you to make sense of your career journey to date. You may find it personally beneficial to have the opportunity to review and reflect upon your career history. This may also help you to plan your future career direction. At the end of the interview, there will be the opportunity for you to identify any career information advice and guidance support you might need now or in the future.

The interview:
- Will take no more than 30 minutes;
- Will be in person or via video call;
- Will be recorded (audio only) and transcribed;
- Will take place at a location that is convenient for you, and if travel expenses are incurred, these will be refunded.

If you have any additional requirements that I can accommodate in the interview, please let me know in advance by email at emma@scottishuniversity.ac.uk.

(Continued overleaf...)

Your data: • Will be anonymised and a pseudonym used; • Will be deleted from the recording device used in the interview and moved to secure, password-protected storage; • Will be deleted upon completion of the research project [SCHEDULED DATE].
What are the possible risks of taking part?
In discussing your career history, you may revisit challenging times in your life or raise sensitive points. You may feel uncomfortable or emotional when considering these times in your life. If you do not wish to share specific details at any point, we will move on, and I will deal with these moments empathetically. This project is based at HERE and commenced in 2014. It has been co-funded by FUNDERS HERE.
Data protection
Your responses to this survey are confidential and will be used only by the researcher, Emma Bolger, who is employed by the University of Scotland. Your responses are confidential and will be used only as part of this research project. You can withdraw your participation in the survey if you no longer wish to take part. Emma can be contacted at emma@scottishuniversity.ac.uk if you have any questions about the survey. This study has been approved by the Research Ethics Committee at the University of Scotland. You will never be publicly identifiable by your answers and all data collected will be used and stored securely in line with the UK GDPR and the Data Protection Act (2018). Any ethical or other concerns relating to this survey can be realised with to the University Data Controller who can be contacted by email at: datacontroller@scottishuniversity.ac.uk
Thank you
Thank you for your interest and participation in my project.

Template for a participant informed consent form

Informed consent

Project title	

Please read the following statements and, if you agree, mark the corresponding box to confirm agreement.

I confirm that I have read and understand the information sheet	
I have had the opportunity to consider the information and ask questions	
I understand that my participation is voluntary and that I am free to withdraw at any time without giving any reason	
I consent to the processing of my personal information relating to my career history for the purposes explained to me	
I understand that such information will be handled in accordance with all applicable data protection legislation	
I understand that my data will be treated confidentially and any publication resulting from this work will report only data that does not identify me	
I agree to having my voice digitally recorded	
I freely agree to participate in this research interview	

Interviewee	Researcher
Your Name	Researcher name
Signature	Signature

Interview details
Date of interview:
Location of interview:

Template for a survey title page (including informed consent and participant information)

Survey or project title
About the survey
Introduce the purpose of the survey and research project.
Clarify who should complete the survey (your target sample).
Survey summary
Give an overview of the content.
Estimate of how long it should take to complete the survey.
Highlight any potential benefits or risks to the participant of completing the survey.
Consent
State that responses to the survey are confidential and how their data will be used.
Include your full name, and if relevant, a description of who you are.
State that participants are free to withdraw at any point.
Alternative formats
Offer the survey in an alternative format (it may be helpful to state what format that will be, for example, on paper, or if you would like to complete it over the phone)
Ethics and data protection
Explain how the data obtained will be used and managed.
Include your contact details.
Include named third party contact details (obtain authorisation from someone other than yourself in a reasonable position of authority to be named here).

An example survey title page

Apprenticeships in healthcare

This survey is part of a university lecturer's research project into apprenticeships.

This survey is for young people aged 16–25 who are currently completing an apprenticeship and working in healthcare in Scotland.

You will be asked about your experience of doing an apprenticeship, and the survey should take you no more than five minutes to complete. By completing this survey, you can be entered into a prize draw to win a gift voucher.

Your responses to this survey are confidential and will be used only by the researcher, Emma Bolger, who is employed by the University of Scotland. Your responses are confidential and will be used only as part of this research project. You can withdraw your participation in the survey if you no longer wish to take part. Emma can be contacted at emma@scottishuniversity.ac.uk if you have any questions about the survey.

If you would like the survey in an alternative format (e.g. on paper, or if you would like to complete it over the phone), please email emma@scottishuniversity.ac.uk.

This study has been approved by the Research Ethics Committee at the University of Scotland. You will never be publicly identifiable by your answers and all data collected will be used and stored securely in line with the UK GDPR and the Data Protection Act (2018). Any ethical or other concerns relating to this survey can be realised with to the University Data Controller who can be contacted by email at: datacontroller@scottishuniversity.ac.uk

Please click on 'Next' to start the survey.

Poster reading directions

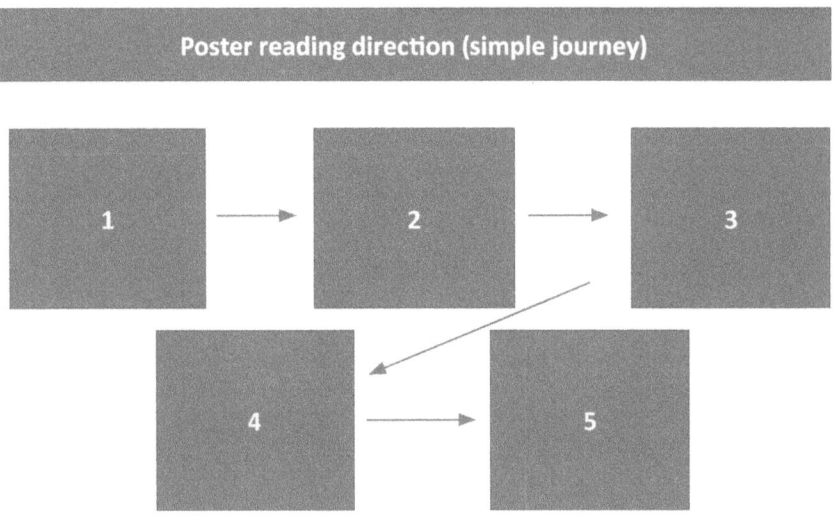

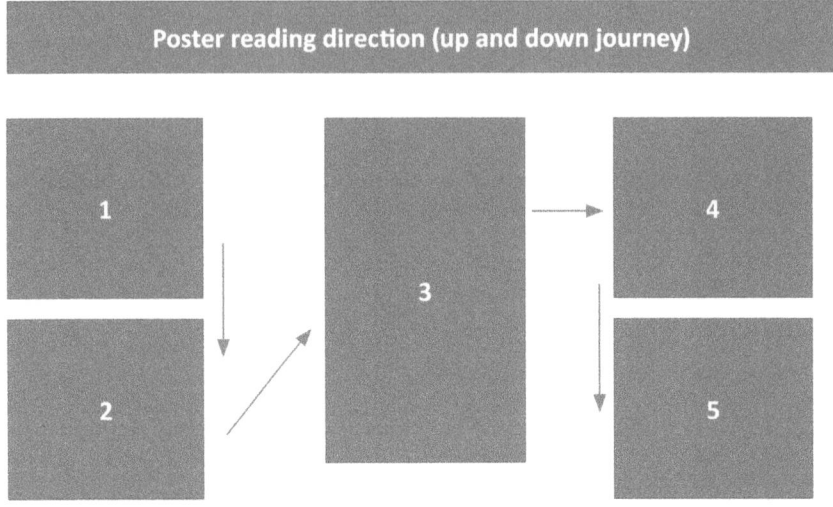

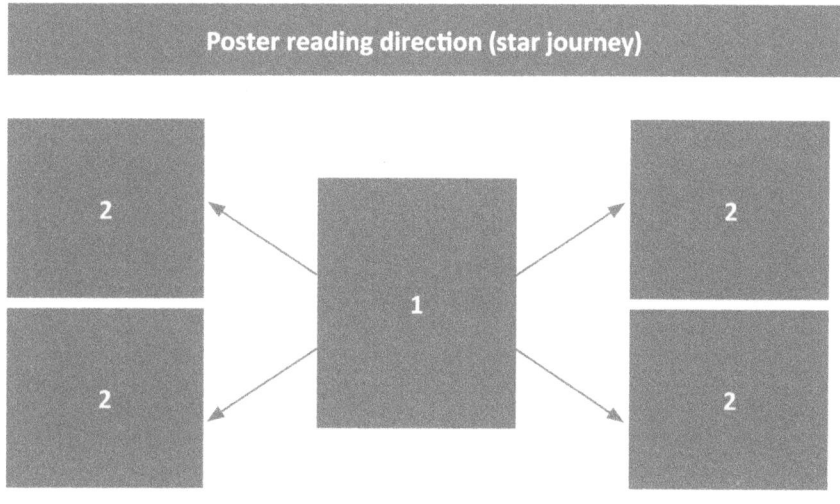
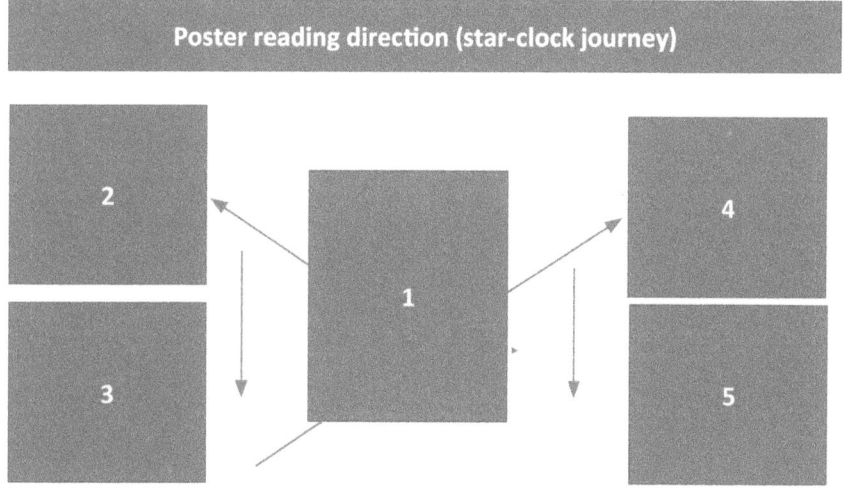

www.ingramcontent.com/pod-product-compliance
Lightning Source LLC
Chambersburg PA
CBHW061753290426
44108CB00029B/2984